Self-Worth and School Learning

Martin V. Covington
University of California, Berkeley

Richard G. Beery
University of California, Berkeley

Holt, Rinehart and Winston
New York, Chicago, San Francisco, Atlanta, Dallas,
Montreal, Toronto, London, Sydney

Library of Congress Cataloging in Publication Data

Covington, Martin, 1938-
  Self-worth and school learning.

  (The Principles of Educational Psychology Series)
  Bibliography: p. 149
  Includes index.
  1. Educational psychology.   2. Self-respect.   I. Beery,
Richard G., joint author.   II. Title.   [DNLM: 1. Learn-
ing.   2. Self concept.   3. Psychology, Educational.
LB1051 C873s]
LB1051.C696   370.15   76-2052
ISBN 0-03-015286-0

Foreword

The Principles of Educational Psychology Series

The materials used to present educational psychology to teachers should have two dominant characteristics—excellence and adaptability. The *Principles of Educational Psychology Series* aspires to both. It consists of several short books, each devoted to an essential topic in the field. The authors of the books are responsible for their excellence; each author is noted for a command of his or her topic and for a deep conviction of the importance of the topic for teachers. Taken as a whole, the series provides comprehensive coverage of the major topics in educational psychology, but it is by no means a survey, for every topic is illuminated in a distinctive way by the individual approach of each author.

Numerous considerations require that the materials used for instruction in educational psychology be adaptable. One consideration is that the readership is heterogeneous, including students in pre-service teacher training programs, of whom some have and others have not taken prior work in psychology, as well as professional teachers in in-service programs who have already completed previous courses in educational psychology. The separate booklets in the *Principles of Educational Psychology Series* are intended to be responsive to these differences. The writing is clear and direct, providing easy access for the novice, and the authors' fresh and distinctive viewpoints offer new insights to the more experienced.

Another consideration is that the format of courses in educational psychology varies widely. A course may be designed for pre-service or for in-service programs, for early childhood, elementary, secondary, or comprehensive programs, or to offer special preparation for teaching in urban, suburban, or rural settings. The course may occupy a full academic year, a semester, trimester, quarter, or an even shorter period. A common set of topics may be offered to all students in the course, or the topical coverage may be individualized. The *Principles of Educational Psychology Series* can be adapted to any one of these formats. Since the series consists of separate books, each one treating a single topic, instructors and students can choose to adopt the entire set or selected volumes from it, depending on the length, topical emphasis, and structure of the course.

The need for effective means of training teachers is of increasing urgency. To assist in meeting that need, the intent of the series is to provide materials for presenting educational psychology that are distinctive in approach, excellent in execution, and adaptable in use.

William Rohwer
Carol Rohwer
Series Editors
Berkeley, California

Preface

Self-Worth and School Learning demonstrates the power of combining theory with practice in organizing, understanding, and dealing with the problems of the student in the classroom. Without practical experience, theory alone may be insufficient to point the way toward constructive solutions; while without theory, classroom innovations—however creative—may lack clear direction and testable implications. A melding of these two can provide impetus for change as well as guideposts for the directions such changes should take. The authors of this book first approached this common juncture from different backgrounds and perspectives, subsequently collaborating to bring together theory with practice in a manner that enriches both.

Dr. Beery's contribution to this effort has been largely from the theoretical perspective. As a psychologist with the Counseling Center at the University of California, Berkeley, Dr. Beery has long been interested in fear of failure among students—particularly as this fear causes maladaptive reactions in the academic endeavor. The basic conceptualizations that resulted originated primarily from intensive individual counseling interviews with students experiencing stress in the educational experience. These discussions, combined with a review of the existing theoretical and experimental literature, led to the development of a comprehensive model, which incorporates a wide variety of student strategies into the common motivational framework of failure-avoidance.

Central to this model is the postulate that students are motivated to enhance, or at least to protect, a belief in their possession of a subjectively satisfying level of intellectual ability. For many, this motive seems to stem from an implicit link between ability and a sense of personal worth. Given such an internalized assumption, avoidance of ability-threatening experiences naturally assumes powerful importance. Combining this motivational assumption with the cognitive perspective of attribution theory, a wide variety of failure-avoidant strategies can be seen as attempts to avert negative ability attributions, sometimes even at the expense of external performance itself.

Since 1970, Dr. Beery has presented his ideas in a number of lectures, seminars, and workshops to groups of undergraduates, graduates, faculty, student service personnel, and the public at large. The theoretical development was particularly aided by substantive student input in two undergraduate psychology seminars that Dr. Beery led on "Fear of Failure in the Student Experience." Grateful acknowledgement is due to these seminar participants and, perhaps most of all, to the many student counselees who so actively shared their personal experiences and perspectives. Further development of the implications Dr. Beery has drawn from this work may be found in two theoretical articles and a forthcoming book on the topic.

Professor Covington's contribution to this effort originates from a somewhat different set of experiences. His long-standing research interests have centered on the development of instructional systems that enhance classroom learning, promote creative thinking, and foster self-confidence and satisfaction in the learner. He has conducted extensive research at both the elementary school level and with college adults. The most recent phase of his research with college students was the creation of the Berkeley Teaching-Learning Project in 1971 to study the effectiveness of various innovative course structures and alternative grading methods among students of differing personality characteristics. The program of research centers around a large-enrollment, introductory psychology class that Professor Covington teaches annually. Special attention has focused on experiments using such techniques as contract grading, absolute evaluative standards, and self–goal-setting among students. Of particular interest has been an analysis of the impact of these different techniques on students who prefer to achieve autonomously as contrasted to those who rely heavily on the instructor for guidance and support.

The Teaching-Learning Project has provided a rich

source of research findings, instructional materials, and practical experience with a wide variety of teaching modalities. Many of the possibilities for classroom learning structures described in this book have evolved from data gathered from this project. Much of the success of this enterprise is owed to the enthusiastic participation of many dedicated graduate students who over the years have met regularly with Professor Covington in an on-going graduate seminar and who have assisted in every phase of the research process as well as in the administration and assistant teaching of the introductory course. The contributions of the following students have been invaluable: Nick Fedan, Bob Kahn, Ted Kahn, Allen Kanner, David Katzenellenbogen, Herschel Kwinter, Ray Launier, Georgina La Russa, Carol Omelich, Alan Schnur, and Mike Spratt. Special appreciation goes to Professors Keith Jacoby and Helgola Ross and to Drs. Jeffrey Martin and Steven Polsky —the original group of graduate assistants who have since received their doctorates and gone on to promising careers in research and teaching.

In 1973, Professor Covington invited Dr. Beery to present his theoretical formulations on fear of failure to the Teaching-Learning seminar as the first step in a proposed collaborative endeavor. The possibilities for dovetailing this conceptual framework with the on-going process of classroom innovation and research became immediately apparent and generated enthusiastic participation and continuing dialogue on the issues. The following academic term, the authors co-led the seminar, which by then was redirected toward the combined goals of joining theory and research in the practical educational setting and generating differential predictions on a number of crucial learning issues. The results already have shown promise of leading to some major breakthroughs in our understanding of classroom dynamics, particularly in the burgeoning area of attributional research, with much of the data still forthcoming.

This book, then, reflects a combination of theory and

practice, interwoven with a broad survey of existing and continuing research. The book was written by Professor Covington and incorporates the results of an extensive literature review on his part with the theoretical elaborations developed by Dr. Beery. The book first looks at differential motivations of students in the classroom, whether success-oriented or failure-avoidant. This discussion is followed by research drawn from a wide range of sources. Finally, some concrete suggestions are proposed for structural change in the teaching enterprise. These suggestions are aimed at the goal of minimizing threat to students while maintaining overall quality and encouraging each student to achieve to his full individual potential.

Grateful acknowledgement is made to Professors Richard Crutchfield, Robert Olton, and Rhona Weinstein for critically reviewing an earlier draft of the manuscript.

Finally, a note regarding the gender of the personal pronouns and their possessives, which appear throughout the book: in the singular case, the masculine form is used rather than the more cumbersome he/she or his/her construction. This is done for the sake of simplicity and readability and is meant to imply nothing about the sex of the students and teachers described.

Martin V. Covington
Richard G. Beery
Berkeley, California
January 1976

Contents

Chapter 1   Introduction and Overview

An Introductory View

Several thousand years ago a social critic chronicled the sad plight of Greco-Roman society and in particular the failure of its educational system. "Our students have grown lazy," he wrote, "and are disrespectful of authority. They slight their tutors, mislead their teachers, and fail to attend to their lessons. Students criticize one another excessively, and are equally ill-disposed toward their own efforts. And not surprising—schools are little more than jails . . . where masters ridicule pupils, flog and beat them without reason, and make light of the smallest errors."

We can surmise from these pointed remarks that the educational enterprise in western culture has been in trouble for a long time. Indeed, these comments have an uncomfortably contemporary ring. Some things seem to have changed little in the intervening centuries—student apathy, indifference to learning, and wasted talent. For instance, it is sobering to realize that today in some of our cities the rate of student deaths caused by violence and drug overdose approaches the rate of American combat fatalities in World War II; that 15 percent of our ghetto students never complete the eighth grade; and that among high school graduates average reading proficiency is below the ninth grade level. To be sure, in many respects the quality of school life has vastly improved over an earlier day: corporal punishment has slowly been eliminated as a method of student control, physical surroundings are more conducive to learning, and education has been so democratized that more people have access to learning today than was ever imagined possible by previous generations. Moreover, our understanding of the educational process itself has steadily increased, but then so have the "stakes" in terms of human survival. We can ill afford the continued disruption and waste of human talent on such a vast scale when so much hangs in the balance.

Today education is a vital part of our hope for the future as human beings find themselves struggling with the most basic issues of their existence: how to become part of the balancing force in nature rather than continuing to exploit the environment for short-term gain; how to replace war as the habitual method for achieving peace; and how to make the wisest use of powerful new biochemical techniques with their awesome ability to change a person's capacities and his very nature.

From an educational perspective what is even more worrisome than the problems themselves is the fact that many of them were undreamt of only a few decades ago. Thus it is that in their turn the present generation of young people will have to deal with problems that today are largely unforeseen. This is only too clear from the current "knowledge explosion." Knowledge makes so much possible. In fact, new knowledge has always been the key to solving existing problems, but these solutions invariably are accompanied by new and unexpected difficulties. As only one timely example of this, the technology of the twentieth century made possible the building of the Aswan Dam, which, it was hoped, would create productive farmlands out of thousands of square miles of Egyptian desert. Yet this particular solution to the problem of hunger in the eastern Mediterranean now threatens the entire region with ecological disaster: severe erosion of the Nile River Basin, a breakdown of the aquatic food chain in the Mediterranean Sea, a rising salt level that threatens to sterilize the rich Nile soil, and the aggravation of various public health problems. On balance it appears that rather than alleviating the problem of hunger, this solution has only aggravated it.

The sense of dislocation that results from this flood tide of knowledge and rapidly changing values has become so familiar to us that it has been given a label: *future shock!* The phenomenon of future shock places an unprecedented burden on our educational system, one that the schools are largely unprepared to accept. The most obvious problem is that there is simply *more* to know in order to remain literate and functional in today's society, and from all indications this burden of knowledge will continue to increase at an ever-accelerating rate. However, if this were the only difficulty, schools could continue to cope in much the same ways they always have—for above all else, schools are best equipped to dispense facts, and students remain obligingly ready to memorize them. Solutions would simply involve making learning more rapid and efficient, for example, through computer-assisted instruction or by increasing the number of years individuals spend in school. But an abundance of facts is not the only problem, nor is it the most important. Future shock also forces upon us the realization that knowledge is not only expanding but is subject to increasingly rapid change as well. Today the life of some facts—the time before they become obsolete—can be counted in terms of months or even days. One college instructor put it best when he recently told his students, "Half of what I will tell you is true; the other half, false and misleading. The problem is that no one can *yet* tell which is which!"

Schools do not prepare students to cope with this kind of change and with the unknown quality of the future. Yet if our youth are to lead satisfying personal lives as adults and contribute to the public good, they must be capable of reassessing their beliefs and values in light of a vastly altered world. For this reason their education must be founded on systematic instruction in *how* to think rather than *what* to think.

Yet schools must do even more than train students in the capacity to think, and this brings us to the heart of the matter. Schools must also foster a *will* to learn and to relearn; in effect, they must develop a capacity for lifelong self-renewal. Students must be encouraged to believe in themselves and in the validity of their own thought processes. In addition, they must develop a sense of personal effectiveness, that is, the conviction that they control their own destiny and cause their own achievements. Lord Kenneth Clark reminds us that the great ages of history and civilization were times of supreme confidence:

> . . . civilisation requires a modicum of material prosperity —enough to provide a little leisure. But, far more, it requires confidence—confidence in the society in which one lives, belief in its philosophy, belief in its laws, and confidence in one's own mental powers. . . . Vigour, energy, vitality: all the great civilisations—or civilising epochs—have had a weight of energy behind them (1969, p. 4).

Likewise, epochs of regression and darkness are anticipated by a decline in corporate self-respect; despair does not convene parliaments nor launch voyages of exploration. And so it is with individuals as well.

The challenge is clear. Not only must schools accelerate the acquisition of knowledge, but they must do it in such a way that students become the masters—not the prisoners— of their knowledge and have the confidence to transform it to their own purposes. It is in this sense—the one that is significant—that teachers must foster both confidence *and* high achievement in their students. Happily, these two goals are not incompatible; in fact, they are mutually interdependent. Self-esteem is not something separate from performance but rather integral to it. It is through achievement that academic self-confidence grows, and increased confidence in turn promotes achievement through inspiring further learning. In short, confidence and competence must increase together for either to prosper. When they do not grow apace, students are likely to suffer. We will soon see how disastrous the consequences are of attaining high academic goals without a firm base in personal confidence. The ultimate example of this is the compulsive *overstriver* who accomplishes much—not because he is motivated to succeed, but because he is afraid to fail. Conversely, it is difficult to maintain self-esteem in the absence of satisfying personal accomplishments. While *underachievers* may appear to do this for a time, their inflated self-regard is illusory and sustained by extraordinary defensive mechanisms.

Teaching for a *will* to learn is no easy task. The evidence of this abounds in the form of massive student disaffection, anger, and mediocre performance. This book argues that many such negative reactions toward school have a common origin. Often they are reactions to threat—a threat to the student's sense of worth. In the remainder of this first chapter we will sketch in the broad outlines of this argument. First, we will consider the concept of self-worth, then describe the nature of the threat, and finally explore how this threat may lead to poor performance and to low academic motivation.

Overview of the Problem

Self-worth

Self-worth is the individual's evaluative appraisal of himself. In the broadest sense it is more or less synonymous with such concepts as self-esteem, self-respect, and personal acceptance. Naturally the individual acts to protect his sense of worth when it is threatened. In fact, these protective efforts seem so universal that many psychologists have assumed the need for self-aggrandizement to be a primary motive animating much of human behavior (see Epstein, 1973). Basically these experts agree that the individual attempts to maximize success, which enhances a sense of worth, and to avoid failure, which threatens to devalue it.

The Threat

The individual's sense of worth is threatened by the belief that his value as a person depends on his ability to achieve, and that if he is incapable of succeeding, he will not be worthy of love and approval (Beery, 1971). This is not an incomprehensible belief. There is a tendency in our society to equate achievement with human worth; in effect, people are held to be only as good as their socially-valued achievements. Indeed, some researchers (e.g., Rosenberg, 1965) have found that no single thing contributes as much to the student's sense of esteem as does a good report card, nor shatters it so profoundly as do poor grades. This kind of reaction is inevitable in a society like ours where a primary determinant of one's status is the ability to perform.

This preoccupation with ability and performance begins surprisingly early in life. Most five year olds can already identify the brightest and dullest among their peers and often point out the differences with relish. Moreover, these youngsters seem firmly convinced that ability is the main ingredient in achieving success and that a lack of ability is the reason for failure. And, according to the harsh logic of childhood morality, it is widely held that success is the only legitimate basis for giving rewards. Having tried hard is no particular virtue and should go unrewarded. To these young children it is only the outcome that counts! Although this strict attitude mellows somewhat with age (Weiner and Peter, 1973)—and student *effort* and good intentions begin to count for more—it is still *outcome* and its handmaiden, *ability*, that dominate as the supreme virtues right on into adulthood. Little wonder then that we find among older students of high school and college age a tendency to devalue successes that occur through hard work, while successes achieved in the absence of effort are highly regarded (Beery, 1974, 1975; Covington and Omelich, 1975).

Given all this, it is understandable that ability so often becomes confused with worth. To be *able* is to be *worthy*, but to do poorly seems evidence of inability and thus reason to despair of one's worth. For those who are insecure or low in self-esteem, anchoring a sense of worth on ability is a risky step. This is largely because schools, as we shall see, can easily threaten a student's belief in his own ability.

Threat and Poor Performance

School offers the first major opportunity outside the home for a child to test his abilities and to gain admiration and respect. This may work well for most of those who are successful in school—success reinforces the pursuit of excellence and leads to an increasing sense of competency. But what of those who fail to attain the expectations of their teachers and parents or, most importantly, of themselves? These students may come to blame themselves for failure and attribute it to a lack of ability. Naturally, this is highly threatening. Out of such anguish and frustration a fateful decision is often made, unwittingly and without regard for the consequences. In essence, the student may reason that if he cannot be sure of succeeding, then at least he can protect his dignity by avoiding the experience of failure, with its implications for demoting his belief in his ability. Thus there emerge in schools two fundamentally different, widespread patterns of achievement motivation: one with an orientation toward success and the other, an attempt to avoid a sense of failure (see Atkinson and Litwin, 1960).

The fundamental difference between these two dispositions is reflected in the different interpretations students give to their successes and failures. Consider first the success-oriented student. Success is usually taken as evidence of ability—if a person did well on previous occasions, presumably he has the capacity to do well again. For this reason the success-oriented student steadily gains confidence in his abilities and comes to see himself as equal to most school tasks. Consequently, when he encounters failure, he is most likely to blame it on insufficient effort. This interpretation is all-important because it robs failure of its threat! Here failure does not necessarily reflect on ability. Moreover, it is something that can be set right by trying harder. In other words, failure is viewed as an inevitable and natural part of the learning process and not as a characteristic of the learner. Because of this, success-oriented students are willing to run reasonable risks of failure— risks that are necessary to achieve. They focus on the challenges of the learning task rather than being distracted by worry and self-doubt, and they take credit for their triumphs and accept responsibility for poor performance. All these qualities—a sense of responsibility, personal control over events, and confidence in one's own ability—combine to produce an attitude of hope and trust in the future and in life generally. Hope is both a prerequisite to successful action and a consequence of it. It is the difference between the one student who says he "expects to do poorly in school," and the other who "hopes to do well."

While the pursuit of excellence for its own sake is liberating and constructive, an escape from failure breeds anxiety, apathy, and often, self-defeat. The student who is failure-avoiding harbors secret doubts about his ability, and ability seems a vital commodity to him, linked as it is to his sense of self-worth. Fearing he lacks sufficient ability, he despairs of succeeding well enough in the future, especially since he has it on good authority from older brothers and sisters that school gets harder rather than easier. Faced with a situation where failure threatens to rob him of his respect, this student has little choice but to maneuver to avoid failure, even if it means hindering his chances for success. As we shall see, a number of ingenious strategies are available for this purpose. One common ploy is simply not to participate. However, since teachers severely penalize not trying, some effort is usually called for—just enough to avoid punishment yet not so much that the student must assume responsibility for failure should it occur. For if he tried too hard and still failed, the implication would go to low ability. So he works just enough to get by. This kind of strategy leads to a school record of mediocre accomplishment. On the one hand, the student has no clear failures and has protected himself should failure occur, but, on the other hand, his grades give him little cause for pride. And what of those situations when the student expects to fail no matter how hard he tries? Here still other defensive strategies may come into play. If the student cannot avoid failure per se, then he can at least attempt to avoid a *sense* of failure in the face of this inevitable outcome. Procrastination is a prime example. To be sure, by putting things off until too late the student sets up his own failure, but he does so in such a way as to avoid the shameful implication that he lacks ability. He can now attribute failure to other things and argue, in effect, that his poor performance is not representative of what he can really do and therefore is not a fair measure of his ability and even less of his worth. In short, this becomes a kind of "failure with honor."

The irony of all this is that by his own actions the failure-avoiding student may actually set up overt failure in his desperate attempts to avoid *feelings* of failure. Thus this student becomes his own worst enemy. He continues to harbor doubts about his ability because he is unwilling to test his limits by trying his hardest. He fears that he *might* be inadequate, but what he fears even more is finding out. Tragically, such students not only fail to enhance their sense of worth or ability but end up performing well below their actual level of competency. These self-deceptions are easy to begin but difficult to reverse because they carry a momentum of their own. Once they are used, it is that much easier to rely on them again in the face of recurring threat. Such concessions and retreats from reality—minor as well as major—leave a residual of self-doubt that accumulates and undercuts the chances for future success.

Causes of Failure-Avoidance

Defensive maneuvering becomes necessary largely because many classrooms are failure-oriented. That is, they provide insufficient rewards for *all* students to strive for success; too many youngsters must struggle simply to avoid punishment. This tragic fact and the processes behind it are far too complex and dynamic to be considered in a static fashion. It is best, therefore, to proceed with the aid of a model of classroom dynamics that reflects the ever-changing interactions between teachers, students, and resulting success and failure. Yet this analysis must take place within manageable limits for if we try to pay attention to everything, we will understand nothing.

A promising approach to the questions of how and why rewards become limited is provided by Alfred Alschuler (1973a), who distinguishes between what we shall call failure-prone classrooms and achievement-oriented classrooms. Basically, Alschuler views the dynamics of classroom learning as a complex game—a kind of learning game. While this analogy to classroom learning is not strictly true, the parallel is striking enough to provide us with some important insights. Like all popular games, the classroom situation can be analyzed in terms of formal properties. First, there is the *scoring system* by which players (students) receive points (rewards). Second, there are *obstacles* that must be overcome to gain points. And third, there is the matter of who makes up the rules and enforces them.

Consider the failure-oriented classroom. These classrooms elicit a power struggle in which students compete with one another for a fixed number of rewards to be divided in unequal ways. This is, in effect, a zero-sum scoring system. When one player makes points, others automatically lose points. This is most clearly seen in the case of competitive grading—or, as it is commonly called, "grading on the curve"—in which a few students succeed at the expense of everyone else. According to Alschuler, in such a classroom the implicit goal becomes competitive, since one can hope to win only by gaining superiority, influence, and control over others. Such situations, however, produce few winners. Instead students become experts at learning ways to survive. One of these ways is to sabotage the efforts of other students. While this happens infrequently at the elementary level, acts of sabotage become almost epidemic in high school and college where students think nothing of stealing assigned books from the library or ripping out crucial pages in an effort to handicap others. The obstacles to success, then, are other students; they become opponents in the learning game. But usually the biggest opponent of all is the teacher, since it is the teacher who sets up the rules by which students play. As a consequence, the teacher-student relationship is basically power-oriented, with the teacher exercising authority and ascendency over the students.

The net effect of this struggle among competitors—teacher and student alike—is to limit the supply of rewards. This happens for a number of reasons. One is that students tend to judge the quality of their work in terms of how well others are doing, a notoriously poor yardstick for gauging the quality of one's efforts. For instance, a student may deserve praise for a job well done yet reject recognition because he feels he is doing no better than his rivals. Another reason is that in such a competitive climate success becomes valued primarily because of its scarcity. An accomplishment is worth more as a sign of ability and status if only a few attain it. Thus, if the teacher finds something praiseworthy about the work of each student, ironically, the value of his praise may be cheapened owing to its frequency. Ultimately, this shrinking supply of rewards has the effect of pushing the student's aspirations beyond his current reach in order to gain recognition from the teacher who values high achievement.

Students react differently to such pressure. Some choose to compete anyway, despite the inflated standards and as a result experience repeated failure. Others may readjust their sights downward to more realistic goals only to be ridiculed by their peers for not keeping up. Still others may reject the learning game and drop out altogether. But in many ways the student who pays the highest price is the one who attempts to avoid failure by succeeding. More about these different kinds of students later.

From this analysis it seems clear that the structure of classroom learning brings out different kinds of student motivation—in the case just described, a failure-avoiding motive. This is a vital point because it pertains to the whole matter of causation and to the question of what features of school life should be modified in order to enhance competency and feelings of self-worth.

First, let us consider what is *not* a cause of failure-avoidance. For one thing, there is no evidence that the process of learning itself is inherently threatening or distasteful. To the contrary, everything points to learning as a natural and adaptive process. At the same time, stating that resistance to learning is caused by a lack of motivation or low self-regard does not tell us anything. A student who resists learning is often said to be unmotivated, but this is simply another way to describe the difficulty. Calling a student "unmotivated" may *identify* the problem but does not *explain* it, nor does it tell us much about the causes. In short, we must be careful not to confuse descriptions of behavior with their causes. If academic failure becomes a chronic way of life for a student, he will naturally come to regard himself as a poor student and perhaps even worthless. But these attitudes and feelings are not the root cause of his problem, although they will eventually become *part* of the problem. Rather, they are the outcome of whatever conditions led to his lack of success originally. Thus, low motivation, negative self-attitudes, and failure are largely the result of improper learning conditions. According to this learning-theory analysis, we should be able to alter a student's failure rate by changing the conditions of classroom learning and, as a consequence, increase his motivation to succeed. Actually there is considerable experimental evidence on this point, which we shall review later.

This line of argument also serves to place the teacher's role and responsibility in a perspective that differs somewhat from the commonly accepted view. In recent years it has become fashionable to blame teachers for the breakdown in school learning. But a more balanced analysis will show that, in reality, teachers are as much victims of the learning system as they are victimizers. This is not to suggest that there are no stupid, incompetent, or insensitive teachers. We know there *are*. We need only consult any number of contemporary critics of education to find ample and chilling evidence of teacher brutality and viciousness. This ill-suited minority must be replaced if for no other reason than a regard for common decency. But doing this will not entirely solve the problem of the failure-prone student since the root causes lie elsewhere—in the actual structure of school learning. There is considerable subjective testimony from school children on this point (see Jackson, 1968, Ch. 2). Few students express a dislike for their present teachers or for teachers as a group, but what they do not like is school—that is, the institutionalization of learning.

As we shall see, teacher and students are caught up together in a drama with all the elements of a Greek tragedy. Despite the best intentions of all, students are wasted and teachers disillusioned. Teachers want to be respected, to be helpful, and to feel worthy; students, too, want no less. Given such noble and compatible desires, why do things go wrong? The problem stems partly from a conflict of priorities between teacher and students. Above all, teachers value high achievement through effort, while many students are driven to avoid failure and the unpleasant implication that they lack ability. Teachers reward effort because it seems fair—not everyone is able, but everyone can try. Yet for many youngsters expending effort is a threat because if they study hard and still fail, their ability becomes suspect. Consequently when students do not respond to teacher praise with increased effort, teachers become puzzled, sometimes angered, and may even feel betrayed. Though teachers are likely to regard such resistance as a lack of motivation, the student is usually far from unmotivated. To the contrary, he is highly motivated, but for the wrong reasons. He is trying hard to avoid a sense of failure and to protect his feelings of self-worth.

The Structure of this Book

In this brief overview we have provided a summary of the problems inherent in fostering achievement and a sense of self-worth in the schools. This overview should help you to understand more fully the many points to be made in the remainder of the book.

In the next three chapters we will give a more detailed account of the nature of the threat to self-worth, its causes, and consequences. Chapter 2 identifies what it is about the structure of learning that can bring about a scarcity of classroom rewards, causing many students to seek ways to avoid failure rather than strive for success. In Chapter 3 we will look at the various kinds of failure-avoiding strategies and how they can lead to specific maladaptive achievement patterns such as *underachieving* and *overstriving*. In that chapter we will also consider why it is that some children enter school already disposed to avoid failure while others are more hopeful of success. Chapter 4 documents how the continued use of these defensive strategies can cut the student off from an already scarce supply of classroom rewards and how these same strategies also come to crystallize the student's image of himself as a failure. Throughout this chapter two troublesome themes emerge: the irresistible quality of these negative forces and the potential vulnerability of all students to them.

In the second part of the book—Chapters 5, 6, and 7—

we will consider the various ingredients necessary for fostering a sense of self-worth and achievement in an individual. The matter is most constructively stated as a question. To quote John Gardner (1961), founder of Common Cause, "How can we provide opportunities and rewards for individuals of every degree of ability so that individuals at every level will realize their full potentialities, perform at their best and harbor no resentment toward any other level? [p. 115]" The weight of evidence presented in the early chapters is sobering and leaves little doubt either about the importance or the difficulty of answering this question. Indeed, there is no single answer. Rather there are many answers, and each is as specific as the individual student concerned. But whatever form these specific answers take, they are all governed to one degree or another by a set of general principles, which is the subject of the second half of this book.

A Note about References

At the end of each chapter is a list of references pertaining to the topics discussed. These references are meant to provide a further source of material that the interested student can consult. Additionally, specific research studies cited in each chapter are listed in full in the References at the end of the book.

General References

Epstein, S. The self-concept revisited or a theory of a theory. *American Psychologist*, 1973, **28**, 404–16.

Hamachek, D. E. *Encounters with the self*. New York: Holt, Rinehart and Winston, 1971.

Chapter 2   Institutional Causes of Success and Failure

In this chapter we will explore the reasons why schools become instruments of failure for countless students. To present this analysis in both a convincing and a responsible fashion we must first define the twin concepts of *success* and *failure*. All too often schools have been accused by their critics of breeding failure without benefit of a proper definition of terms. We shall see that—psychologically— success and failure depend largely on the student's own standards of achievement and on what he expects of himself; hence, in theory, success and failure are not only properties of the individual but are of his own making as well.

In practice, however, things turn out differently. In the actual school situation students progressively lose control over their own rate of success and may even come to deny themselves the personal satisfaction of a job well done. There are a number of factors in classroom life that contribute to this breakdown. We will explore three: (1) the fact that as personal evaluation becomes official, as it does in schools, the mistakes and errors that are a natural part of the learning process are misinterpreted as failures; (2) the fact that success is often cheapened because students are motivated to work not so much for the sake of learning itself but for extrinsic rewards such as gold stars and grades; and (3) that due to competitive pressure the standards for a successful performance are accelerated beyond the reach of many.

These factors, working in unison, lead to a scarcity of classroom rewards, a condition that forces many students to struggle to avoid failure rather than to seek out success.

Success and Failure

We used two words repeatedly throughout the introductory chapter: *success* and *failure*. Before proceeding, we need to know something of their meaning and how they will be defined here. First, it must be realized that success and failure are psychological concepts—that is, for the most part, there are few objective or public standards for what count as success and failure as there are, for example, in the measurement of height and weight. Success and failure mean different things to different people; indeed, one individual's success can be another's failure, even though their actual accomplishments are identical! Yet for all the subjectivity involved, there *are* some reasonable answers to the question of what constitutes experiences of success and failure.

Level of Aspiration

One of the most important sources of information on success and failure comes from research conducted nearly half a century ago at the University of Berlin by Professor Kurt Lewin and his assistant, Ferdinand Hoppe. Hoppe (as reported in Barker, 1942) presented individuals with a number of simple tasks. One of these required the tossing of sixteen rings onto rapidly moving pegs. After each practice trial Hoppe chatted with his subjects about their progress and asked when it was that they experienced a sense of accomplishment or disappointment. He soon found that actual performance had little to do with these feelings. One person might feel successful after correctly placing only three rings on the pegs, while another might experience considerable disappointment with ten rings correct. Moreover, the achievement level needed for success changed constantly for each individual; a performance that was satisfying on an early trial might be judged as totally inadequate later on. From these observations Hoppe concluded that it is the individual's goals and self-standards that determine feelings of success and failure. Hoppe called a person's self-expectations his *level of aspiration*. This concept has since become an important one in psychology and has been especially influential in research on the fear of failure.

Hoppe's conclusion is central to our understanding of the complex relationships among school achievement, confidence, and a sense of self-worth. In a manner that parallels the laboratory research, success and failure in school also depend on a person's performance relative to his goals and to classroom standards. Briefly stated, when an individual's performance falls below these standards, he experiences a sense of failure and tends to judge himself in critical ways. In contrast, when the individual meets or surpasses the accepted standards, he experiences feelings of success and well-being and judges himself in self-approving ways. Thus in school, as in Hoppe's laboratory, the incidence of success and failure is largely independent of *actual* performance. This psychological basis for defining success and failure is an important point to keep in mind as we proceed.

This analysis also helps us with another elusive concept

—self-confidence. By and large, it can be said that a person is confident of success when he sees himself as equal to the task and less confident to the extent he believes himself unable to attain the prevailing standards. Basically, then, confidence is the individual's subjective estimate of success. Naturally, in specific situations the individual's degree of confidence will vary widely, depending on such things as the perceived difficulty of the task and on how well he feels he should do. In contrast, the more general expression of confidence—in the form of either hope or despair of the future—is a relatively stable, enduring characteristic of the individual that slowly evolves through encountering success and failure in numerous situations.

Self-regulated Success

Hoppe (as reported in Barker, 1942) also studied the effects that success and failure had on his subjects' subsequent goal-setting behavior. After a success, individuals would typically raise their levels of aspiration and, conversely, after a failure, they would lower them. (Subsequent investigators have coined the phrase "typical shift" to describe this sensible strategy.) In effect, most individuals tend to alter their levels of aspiration so as to maintain a reasonable balance between the incidence of success and failure. Because of this, Hoppe interpreted the level of aspiration as a protective mechanism—a kind of check and balance device—that allows individual protection against the possibility of repeated failure and the loss of self-confidence that results. This is achieved by lowering one's self-imposed standards after failure. At the same time, raising expectations after success insures that our accomplishments are gratifying. Although it is true that we seldom tire of success, it is not the easy victory or the "sure thing" that satisfies us, for the easy achievement quickly loses its reward value. Rather it is the accomplishment that involves some element of risk that is valued most. Only by risking failure can success have any real meaning. This tendency to push one's aspirations above present achievement levels has been noted by numerous researchers over the years (see Gould, 1939) and is thought to occur in part from a natural drive for competency. But almost certainly other more ominous factors are at work, too, primarily social pressure to do what is most highly admired without regard for one's actual ability. We will have a good deal more to say about such pressure shortly.

In sum, then, aspirations are a compromise between two opposing tendencies: the need to set expectations low enough to avoid repeated failure yet high enough to gain social approval and to strive for something better. Maintaining a balance between these forces is critical if both achievement and confidence are to be sustained. When individuals are free to shift their expectations in accord with their past successes and failures, the resulting aspirations are near the upper bounds of current ability. The net effect of this is that aspirations spiral upward ahead of current achievement, but not so far ahead that these temporary goals cannot be reached and surpassed through persistent effort and practice. The dynamic interplay between and among the setting of personal goals, success and failure, and resulting achievement is astutely described by James Diggory (1966):

If [the individual] chooses an activity which he never attempted before, his first attempts will be purely exploratory. . . . [But] once this exploration ends and he begins a more or less systematic attempt to produce something, he very likely will set implicit or explicit aspirations for his successive attempts; then he can define success or failure. He seldom needs anyone to tell him when he succeeds or fails because he sets his own standards of performance. At first these standards are likely to be modest, relatively easy to achieve, but he moves always towards standards more difficult to achieve. The standards he uses are quite varied and may change from one attempt to the next. Now he tries to produce a result as good as the last one, but quicker. Next, he may disregard time altogether and try to improve the product.

Later he may concentrate on the smoothness of the process and attempt to swing elegantly through a well-ordered and efficient routine. He may discover and invent new processes or adapt new materials or new methods of work. To the casual uninterested observer this may all seem repetitive and dull, but the operator, the worker, may be intensely interested because he never has exacted the same goal on two successive trials. . . . By this process of gentle spurring himself to successively higher achievements, he approaches mastery of himself and his environment. . . . Things like this happen occasionally to most of us. Sometimes they happen without warning or without previous intent on our part, and we discover only retrospectively that we have spent time improving ourselves and our work, completely oblivious of our surroundings or of the passage of time, trapped in the pathway to mastery [pp. 125–26].

Breakdown of Individual Goal Setting

As Diggory observes, this process of self-mastery occurs only occasionally. This is tragic enough, but what is even more troublesome is that, infrequent as they are, these episodes are even less likely to be experienced in school. Indeed, the mood evoked by Diggory of being gently ensnared by the drama of mastering one's environment is largely foreign to the school experience. Why is this? What is it about schools that discourages self-regulated learning of the kind described by Diggory and researched by Hoppe? Basically there are three sources of inhibition: the all-consuming atmosphere of personal evaluation in schools; excessive reliance on extrinsic rewards to motivate learning; and the fact that standards of success and failure are determined largely by someone other than the student himself.

Pervasive evaluation. The kind of evaluation that accompanies self-regulated learning is private and unofficial. Individuals can make mistakes, learn from them, and try again, all in a matter-of-fact way. As Diggory points out, no outsider need remind the individual when he succeeds or fails because he has set his own goals. Actually, even the term failure is somewhat inappropriate here. Whenever a person tries something for himself, a temporary setback is perceived more as a *nonsuccess* than as a failure, that is, the person has temporarily fallen short of a goal, and has not fallen short as a person. It is only when evaluation becomes official and public, as it does in school, that making mistakes comes to elicit feelings of self-blame and humiliation.

The dominant impression of students is that schools are first and foremost places of evaluation, not of learning. Nowhere else in society is the individual scrutinized for so long a time or as intensely as he is in school. This scrutiny usually takes the form of constant testing and examinations. The fact that school tests are notoriously prone to errors of measurement and to misinterpretation by teachers is lost on the impressionable child; all he knows is that tests must be important because testing takes up so much time! What is lost in test precision is made up for by the frequency of testing. Moreover, as Roger Barker points out (1942), adults have alternative sources of gratification such as clubs, church, and unions so they can balance failures in one area against successes in another and thereby maintain self-respect. Not so with the young student. Apart from home and friends, school is the child's major source of approval, and failure there is not easily compensated for.

Extrinsic motivation. When the child reaches school age, much of what he is already learning as part of a natural inclination to master his environment becomes subject to an elaborate system of *extrinsic* rewards involving teacher praise, gold stars, and grades. This causes a change in the motivational basis of learning. Students begin to strive for goals that are unrelated to the act of learning. Consequently there is a shift away from what psychologists refer to as *intrinsic* reinforcers such as self-praise or the joy of learning for its own sake. Ironically, this progression from *intrinsic* to *extrinsic* motivation is just the opposite of what educators hope to accomplish.

In a series of fascinating studies using nursery school children, Mark Lepper and David Greene (1973) have shown how doling out rewards can backfire. In one study these investigators rewarded a group of children for working on several puzzles by giving them an opportunity to play with some attractive toys afterwards. A comparison group received no enticements for playing with these same puzzles. Later, when all the children were free to play with the puzzles or not, as they chose, those youngsters who had come to expect a reward for their efforts spent only half as much time with the puzzles as did the others who had been intrinsically motivated from the beginning. In effect, these researchers had turned play into work!

Psychologically speaking, praise and other forms of extrinsic reinforcement are a kind of payoff for work done. Thus paying a student for what he might otherwise do freely can transform pleasure into drudgery. A humorous anecdote that captures the essence of this principle concerns the old gentleman who was bothered by the noisy play of neighborhood boys (Casady, 1974). How could he get the boys to stop? The old man called the boys together, told them he was quite deaf, and asked that they shout louder so that he might enjoy their fun. In return he was willing to pay each of them a quarter. Needless to say, the boys were delighted to combine business with pleasure, and on that first day the old man got more than his money's worth. On the second day he told the boys that owing to his small pension, he could afford to pay only twenty cents. As the pay rate dwindled day by day, the boys became angry and finally told the old man they would not return. The sly old gentleman had turned play into work and then paid so little that making noise for five cents a day was not worth the effort!

Once school is seen as work, it too can become drudgery with the result that students must be paid or bribed and sometimes threatened to perform. More recent research by Lepper and Greene (1975) uncovers yet another facet of this distressing picture. Youngsters who were observed by an adult during their initial play session with the puzzle tasks later showed a marked disinterest in solving these same puzzles when the adult was absent. Here play becomes work presumably because the child had performed more for the satisfaction of the observer—to impress or to please him—than for the personal pleasure derived from solving a challenging problem. Thus, the mere presence of an adult authority (e.g., a teacher) may in itself be enough to undercut the growth of intrinsic motivation. Here is further evidence of the importance of allowing sufficient school time for private, self-regulated learning and of the heavy price paid for continual, official surveillance.

This discussion is not meant to suggest that extrinsic reinforcement has no legitimate place in the schools. Quite to the contrary. A good deal of research—some of which will form the basis for our recommendations in later chapters—clearly demonstrates the crucial role played by extrinsic motivation in the learning process, especially in the early stages of learning. The point is that teachers must be wary of relying on extrinsic rewards as the sole or even the dominant motivating device. Extrinsic rewards should be used sparingly and even then withdrawn as soon as skills are adequately mastered. Only in this way can the exercise of these skills eventually become satisfying in its own right.

Conformity in goal setting. Once in school, the child finds that standards of acceptable performance are usually set by someone else. This heralds a breakdown of the protective mechanism that formed such a central part of Hoppe's thinking. In short, the child loses control over his own learning. Instead, he must try to keep pace with the ever-accelerating standards of his teacher and peer group.

The available evidence suggests that a large if not overwhelming proportion of students of all ages hold unrealistically high self-expectations. This is as true for occupational aspirations as it is for academic ones. For example, it has been estimated that 80 percent of our youth aspire to high-prestige occupations, which, unfortunately, represent less than 20 percent of the total jobs available to the labor force (Paterson, 1956). There is a similar disparity when it comes to school grades. Far more students aspire to high grades than the grading system permits.

This fact and its consequences for learning and motivation are clearly demonstrated in a study conducted by Esther Battle (1966). Battle studied hundreds of junior high students across a wide intellectual range. Midway through the school year each student was asked to provide several kinds of information including (1) the grades he expected to receive on his next report card and (2) the lowest grades he could receive and still feel satisfied. This latter estimate indicates something of the minimum degree of excellence the student demands of himself, in effect, his standards. It can also be interpreted as the lowest performance level that does not pose a threat to his sense of worth. Battle found that for many of the students interviewed, their standards were higher than the grades they expected to receive. The hoped-for-grade represented more nearly what the student *wished* to attain. But wishful thinking or not, hopes do have a reality, especially disappointed hopes, as can be seen from the resulting data. Those students with unrealistic goals received lower course grades than did a matched comparison group that had the same level of aspiration but whose expectations for achieving these grades were higher. From this, Battle concluded that the difference in grades for the two groups was caused by differences in student confidence. The first group was far less confident because they did not see themselves as equal to the goals they had set, whereas the second group felt more secure in their ability to achieve the same goals.

Incidentally, the process by which *feelings* of confidence are translated into self-confident *behavior* is neatly illustrated in a companion study (Battle, 1965). Students who were more certain of attaining the grades to which they aspired showed greater persistence in working on course assignments. Naturally, working longer and harder increases the likelihood of attaining one's goals, and it is these successes that in turn further increase self-confidence.

Battle's research also serves to underscore another vital point. Unrealistically high standards can occur among students at all intellectual levels. The highly talented student is just as vulnerable to the distress of striving after goals beyond his reach as are less able learners. One is reminded of the brilliant but perfectionist student who bitterly denounces himself for receiving a grade of B+. As noted earlier, feelings of success and failure are psychological events, and as such they depend far more on one's internal standards of excellence than on the actual level of attainment.

In review of this section, we note several factors that act simultaneously to create a breakdown of self-regulated learning. Once the child enters school he progressively loses control: he is told when to learn, how quickly, and whether or not he can feel a sense of accomplishment. Evaluation becomes official and public, leading to feelings of shame and humiliation. Moreover, play becomes work, but, ironically, the wages (successes) are so low that it is not always worth the effort. Yet despite all this, the student holds himself to demanding standards that sometimes prove beyond his present abilities. What, then, are the causes of this continual and often irrational striving?

Rewarding Student Achievement

Students aspire beyond their means because teachers reward high achievement and punish low achievement and so, by the way, does the peer group. Yet teachers cannot be faulted here for they are simply reflecting one of society's most dominant values, the virtue and necessity of high achievement. As already noted, this value permeates the entire structure of society. In fact, when adults are asked to take the part of the teacher in role-playing experiments, they reinforce achievement through a pattern of reward and punishment that is virtually identical to that imposed by teachers themselves (Weiner *et al.*, 1971, p. 98). Interestingly, students, too—even as early as kindergarten—who pretend to be the teacher follow this same pattern (Weiner, 1972, p. 211). Obviously youngsters learn early and well that high achievement gains approval and low achievement, disapproval. It is this tendency to equate worth and achievement that sets the stage for knife-edged competition among students.

And teachers inadvertently fuel this competition in a number of subtle ways. For example, they often devote more of their time and attention to their better students (Felsenthal, 1970; Goldenberg, 1969). Everyone likes a winner, and teachers are no exception. Naturally, they value success and are made uneasy by failure, largely because it may reflect upon their own competency as teachers. In fact, teachers tend to take credit for student success by attributing it to their own teaching skill but are unwilling to accept the blame for student failure (Beckman, 1970; Johnson, Feigenbaum and Weiby, 1964; Omelich, 1974a). As human and understandable as this self-protective tendency is, the net effect is to draw teachers toward more successful students and drive them from mediocre ones.

Of course, students react to these teacher priorities. In order to receive his fair share of recognition, the student must adopt as his own standard the performance of other more successful pupils. In doing so the student is forced to compete against his peers. This phenomenon is most easily seen in the case of below-average students. It has been repeatedly shown that these youngsters set their aspirations well beyond their abilities in a forlorn effort to gain respectability (Anderson and Brandt, 1939; Hilgard, Sait, and Margaret, 1940). Ironically, teachers often mistakenly praise these unrealistic aspirations as evidence of the student's willingness to try. As a consequence, irrational goal setting is unwittingly reinforced. However, unrealistic aspirations are not limited to the poorer students alone. They are frequently found among able students as well. Within any given classroom, students naturally tend to associate with other pupils of like ability and achievement. Thus, within the context of their own particular clique even bright students can see themselves as relatively dull and must strive to keep pace. When such peer groups are artificially created—as in the case of reading groups of different ability levels—the evidence indicates that students tend to hold themselves to standards of performance exhibited by pupils in the more advanced, prestigious groups (Weinstein, 1975).

These two tendencies—teacher preference for superior achievement and student modeling after high-status pupils—combine to create an escalation of group standards that spirals progressively upward, beyond the reach of more and more students. This competitive process becomes intensified in the absence of clear standards for what constitutes acceptable performance. Students, like anyone else, need to know how well they are doing and how much farther they have to go in order to master their lessons satisfactorily. Yet, as psychologist Mary White points out (1968), students are usually unclear about what learning steps remain to be taken. It is also uncommon for students to see examples of the behavior they are expected to produce once learning is completed. Without some objective guidelines supplied by the teacher, students are forced to judge their academic progress and the merit of their achievements against the capricious yardstick of how well others are doing.

Naturally, competitive pressure leads to a deterioration of the relationship between teacher and students, since they become opponents in the learning game. Classroom competition triggers a power struggle between them, with the teacher attempting to exert control over his students by reason of his authority to withhold and dispense rewards. The universal reaction of students is to neutralize this power base by making the teacher's job as difficult as possible. Typically this takes the form of students becoming resistant to learning, a tactic that increases in frequency as the child grows older and wiser. Thus, the stage is set for a constant and often bitter struggle for the student's attention. When the teacher wins, it is called learning; when the student prevails, and thereby avoids learning, it becomes the "discipline problem." Although there is no agreed upon figure for how much class time is wasted in this process, the estimates differ only in degree of pessimism (see Jackson, 1968, Ch. 3).

All too often, the situation deteriorates into a contest between teacher and students in which each side develops strategies in an effort to win. After some two years of intensive observation in urban junior high schools, Alfred Alschuler (1973b; also see Alschuler and Shea, 1974), has drawn up a list of what he believes to be the basic moves and countermoves employed by teachers and students in the "discipline game." A sampler includes:

For teachers:

1. *Waits, stares* (stops lesson)
2. *Tunnel vision:* ignores disruption or does not see it
3. *Making rules:* ordering student to "stop"
4. *Sarcasm, belittling:* "Do you think you can remember if I tell you a fifth time?"
5. *Mini lecture on good and bad behavior and its consequences:* "She wouldn't be bothering you if you did not turn around."

For students:

1. *Getting up:* student gets up to sharpen pencil . . . to throw something in wastebasket . . . to get paper from desk . . .

2. *Noise making* (individual): tapping foot, drumming desk, playing imaginary harmonica, . . . banging teeth with pencil . . .
3. *Solitary escape:* daydreaming, combing hair, pretending to do work, sleeping
4. *Forgetting or not having materials:* "My mother tore it up by mistake."

Teachers and students combine these moves to create actual classroom combat as illustrated by the following example, again from Alschuler (1973b; also see Alschuler and Shea, 1974):

Student: Hey, I forgot my book today. (forgetting)
Teacher: Haven't I told you that everyone should bring their books to class. Without them you can't learn. (mini-lecture)
Student: (aside to peers) I never learn anything in this damn class anyway. (put down)
Teacher: If you don't pay attention to me you'll just have to come in after class. (threat)
Student: (ignores teacher)
Teacher: O.K. Here's a pass for after school. (implements threat)
Student: I won't take this pass and I won't come in after school. (declaration of independence)
Teacher: Go to the office, NOW! (escalation and finis)

If it were not for the underlying tragedy involved, such vignettes and their real-life counterparts would be pure comic. As it is, they illustrate the calamitous ways in which many teachers and students brutalize one another day after day. The student loses because he does not learn, indeed, he comes to hate learning; the teaching staff is victimized by having to spend, according to Alschuler's careful estimate, an average of some 22,000 minutes each year in reprimanding, nagging, and otherwise punishing students.

As Alschuler observes, the problem is not the teacher, nor is it the student. The difficulty lies in the *relationship* between them. Hence, the solution is not to change either the teacher or the student, assuming one or the other to be a troublemaker, but rather to transform the relationship from one of suspicion to one of acceptance and mutual trust. To do this, however, the threat to the student's sense of self-worth must first be reduced. But more about this in later chapters.

If a competitive atmosphere can so easily turn students against teachers, then the relationship among students is also bound to suffer since they too become opponents in the learning game. Aggression and hostility are the inevitable outcomes. These destructive impulses take many forms, not all of them obvious, nor always directly related to academic achievement. In its mildest form, competitiveness is expressed as a constant clamoring for the teacher's attention and approval, often expressed through the violent waving of raised hands whenever the teacher is about to call on someone. This "forest of hands" phenomenon is well known to teachers. How it can subvert learning is neatly illustrated by the classroom observations of Jules Henry (1957):

The children are singing songs of Ireland and her neighbors. . . . While children are singing some of them hunt in the index, find a song belonging to one of the four countries and raise their hands before the previous song is finished in order that they may be called on to name the next song . . . [p. 122].

As Henry points out, singing has become subordinated to the competitive desire of each student to have his song chosen next.

Tattling is another less subtle form of intragroup aggression, as is the constant carping criticism of other students and the merciless laughter at someone else's mistake. But if we can judge from the degree of agitated handwaving, the supreme opportunity for one-upmanship occurs when students are called on to supply the answer to someone who cannot get it on his own. Again, we call on Jules Henry (1957):

Boris had trouble reducing $^{12}\!/_{16}$ to lowest terms, and could get only as far as $^6\!/_8$. . . . Much heaving up and down from the other children, all frantic to correct him. Boris pretty unhappy. Teacher, patient, quiet, ignoring others, and concentrating with look and voice on Boris. . . . After a minute or two she becomes more urgent. No response from Boris. She then turns to the class and says, "Well, who can tell Boris what the number is?" . . . Teacher calls, "Peggy" [p. 123].

Boris's failure provides the opportunity for Peggy to succeed, but at his expense.

The available research evidence regarding competitiveness is not particularly comforting. In the main it suggests that children become increasingly more competitive as they grow older, probably because of the hard lessons learned in school. Linden Nelson and Spencer Kagan (1972) found this age trend when they gave five and ten year olds learning tasks to work on in small groups. The problems were designed so that rewards (toys and other attractive prizes) would be maximized if the children *cooperated* in achieving a joint solution. The ten year olds proved to be far more competitive, even when it was to their advantage to cooperate. In fact, many of them actually forfeited their own chance for rewards in order to deprive others! Among different groups of children tested the worst offenders by far were middle-class Anglo-Americans who were literally cutthroat in their rivalry. Far less competitive were Mexican-American children from low-income families. However, it appears that competition is mainly a property of middle-class values rather than being related to race or cultural background, since Mexican-American children from middle-income families also exhibited a highly competitive spirit. In any event, as Jules Henry notes (1957, p. 128), these findings may help explain why it is that many teachers in middle-class schools are successful at directing the hostility of their students toward one another by reinforcing peer-group competition; while students from lower-income neighborhoods, being more cooperative, often unite in directing their hostility toward the teacher!

In this section we have documented how student competition is often triggered by the very nature of the teacher's educational mission—to ensure high academic performance. Yet while *achievement* is the dominant classroom goal, there is another value that teachers also recognize and seek to reinforce.

Rewarding Student Effort

There is ample evidence that teachers attempt to individualize their treatment of students by praising *effort* as well as high performance. Each of us knows from personal experience that two students who achieve identically may not be rewarded equally. The student who worked hardest will likely be praised the most. This is done to offset *achievement* as the dominant source of approval and also because teachers see student effort as something they can control through the mechanism of reward and punishment (Rest *et al.*, 1973).

At first glance one might suppose that rewarding effort would act to dampen competition and tip the scale of classroom values toward a measure of worth that is within the grasp of all students. But this is not necessarily true. By rewarding effort, teachers unwittingly set up a conflict of values. While the teacher may be willing to praise honest effort, the student is often preoccupied with keeping pace with others. Not that students shun praise for their efforts; to the contrary, they believe it is only fair that teachers recognize effort, especially among those students who are incapable of high accomplishment (Weinstein, 1975). But when it comes to choosing between praise for high *achievement* or praise for sincere *effort*, there is no mistaking which is most valued (Beery, 1974; Covington and Omelich, 1975). Thus it is that while the teacher may laud persistence, effort alone is not sufficiently rewarding for the student. He is just as likely to judge himself inadequate as measured by the stringent, competitive standards of his peer group. When such discrepant evaluations occur, teacher praise does little to increase student self-confidence (Marston, 1968). Even worse, it may actually jeopardize the teacher's credibility. Gergen (1971) notes the tendency among individuals to view their evaluators as untrustworthy if they feel the appraiser has been grossly inaccurate. Apparently this holds true even when the evaluation is highly positive! It matters little that the student's work may actually *be* praiseworthy or that the teacher is acting in the student's best interest. What *does* matter is that the student may discount the teacher's appraisal and come to suspect his motives in praising him.

Politics is not the only profession that must be concerned about the "credibility gap." Teachers must learn to pay more attention to what the student expects of himself before teacher praise can be an effective device for encouraging personal excellence. Praise given to a student who believes he has done a poor job does nothing to relieve his sense of failure and may only strain an already uneasy relationship between teacher and student.

Learning Self-defeating Standards

Not only is there continual pressure on the student to raise his aspirations irrespective of ability, but there are also informal sanctions against lowering them. The most severe of these sanctions is a loss of social acceptability. Rather than risk teacher and peer-group disapproval for being satisfied with unworthy performances, most students tend to hold themselves to austere standards.

The dynamics of this process in the school-age child have been studied extensively by Albert Bandura and his colleagues (Bandura, 1971; Bandura and Kupers, 1964). In the typical experiment a young child observes an adult working on a learning task. The adult sets either high or low standards of performance for himself. As part of the experiment the adult has control over a supply of rewards in the form of candy and toys. Whenever the adult's performance exceeds his self-imposed standards, he generously rewards himself. Conversely, when he fails to attain the standards, he denies himself these trinkets. After observing the adult for several practice trials, the child is permitted to work on the same task. Like the adult before him, the child also has complete control over the rewards (Bandura, 1971, p. 28).

The results of these studies show that children tend to judge their own performances relative to the standards adopted by the adult models, regardless of how difficult these standards are to attain. In fact, children frequently adhere to excessively stringent standards, so stringent that sometimes even the model has difficulty achieving them! These children rarely reward themselves for performances that fall below the adult criteria, and, as a consequence, they experience continual frustration. Even in the face of repeated failure, they cling resolutely to clearly inappropriate standards. Interestingly, such Spartan self-denial is most likely to be maintained under conditions that approximate a competitive atmosphere—that is, when there is a sense of estrangement from the adult model; when there is little or no opportunity to experience standards other than the group norm; and where considerable social recognition is given for holding high self-standards (Bandura, Grusec, and Menlove, 1967).

As Bandura points out (1971, p. 30), this self-denial is particularly ominous considering the fact that the children are completely free to alter their standards. Also alarming is the ease with which such austere standards can be imposed. If maladaptive behavior can be produced so effortlessly in the research laboratory, how much more frightening the prospects are for children in the regular classroom where a whole host of factors combine to preserve self-defeating standards.

The research of Mischel and Liebert (1966) provides us a glimpse of this complex network of social pressure. These researchers show that stringent patterns of self-reward can be passed on from one student to another. Students who observed an adult model reward himself sparingly later transmitted these same stringent expectations to fellow students. It is in such subtle ways as this that group standards are established and maintained even when they may be entirely inappropriate for many of the peer-group members.

The final tragedy of strict, unforgiving self-standards is that they can take on an autonomous life of their own and continue to operate even though their original cause—competitive pressure—may have long since diminished! But why should students needlessly punish themselves by withholding rewards for perfectly reasonable performances, especially if there is no longer pressure to do so? One intriguing possibility is that these stringent self-expectations are maintained by the very criticisms that the student inflicts upon himself for inadequate performance. Although there is some difference of opinion over the exact mechanisms involved (see Aronfreed, 1964), it is generally agreed that severe self-criticism is followed by a sense of relief and a reduction in anxiety. Thus, ironically, self-punishment takes on a reinforcing value in this context. It ends worry, at least temporarily, and in some cases may even lessen social disapproval of poor performance. Self-criticism, especially if voiced in public, often restores favor in the eyes of others. Yet in the long run it is self-defeating. Far from discouraging excessively high standards (the original culprit), self-punishment simply makes these austere standards more tolerable by temporarily relieving the anxiety and guilt they create. In short, self-contempt relieves the burden of failure, while the root cause of failure remains intact.

Bandura (1971, p. 34) describes an unpublished study by Jack Sandler and John Quagliano that illustrates the effectiveness of self-punishment in relieving discomfort. A group of monkeys was taught to avoid a severe electric shock by pressing a bar. But these animals paid a price for their escape. Pressing the bar produced another shock, though one of far less magnitude than the first. Over time, however, the voltage of the self-administered shock was increased until it came to equal that of the shock the monkeys were avoiding. At this point there was nothing to be gained from choosing the self-administered shock over the other, but the monkeys nonetheless continued to press the bar. Even more surprising, after the original shock had been halted, permanently, these monkeys still persisted in this form of self-punishment! Self-criticism in humans may be sustained for much the same reason. Self-blame, which once acted as a source of relief, is continued, even though the original threat may have long since ceased.

Scarcity of Rewards

As the child progresses through school, scholastic achievement gains in importance as the principal source of approval, and students naturally compete for academic recognition. In the process, however, competition acts to limit these rewards so that they *also* become valued for their scarcity. This means that success follows the laws of *commodity theory* (Brock, 1968). Commidity theory states that all other things being equal, the less frequent an event, the more valued and sought after it becomes. This principle has been applied to the analysis of many social phenomena that involve supply and demand. For example, consider the obscenity issue. Howard Fromkin and Timothy Brock (1973) have questioned the traditional wisdom of dealing with pornography by restricting its distribution, for by the very act of censorship we may unwittingly increase the desirability of prurient material by making it scarce.

Certainly *success* is not pornographic, but it *can* corrupt —especially if it is attainable *only* at the expense of others! This reality is well illustrated by the research of Nelson and Kagan (1972), which was described previously (see p. 33). As part of their research on competition these investigators found that students would cooperate in solving problems as long as each child received a reward. But if there were fewer rewards than participants, a conflict of interest arose, and children became antagonistic and competitive. Here we have all the ingredients of a vicious cycle: insufficient rewards breed competitive pressure and, in turn, competition further increases the scarcity of rewards. And, according to commodity theory, as the likelihood of success decreases, its value increases. Such an inflationary spiral occurs because the fewer the number of successes, the more convincing they are as evidence of a student's high ability. For example, Johnny's reputation as a bright boy would be enhanced far more if he were the *only* student singled out for special praise for his work on a class assignment. If the performances of a number of his classmates were also acknowledged, then the task would be seen as a relatively easy one, certainly requiring no extraordinary ability.

Thus, when the value of success comes to depend primarily on scarcity, it inevitably becomes inflated far out of proportion to its importance. Likewise, the importance of failure is also exaggerated and its meaning distorted. One manifestation of this is that the constructive aspects of failure are widely ignored. Astonishingly, many youngsters are unable to give convincing examples of how they might benefit from making mistakes (Covington, 1968). They are simply not used to viewing failure as a helpful, informative experience. Indeed, students generally believe it wrong not to know the answer when the teacher asks a question. Of course, it is one thing not to know by reason of indifference or lack of preparation, but it is quite another to have studied hard and still not comprehend. This should not be a crime, but students act as if it is. Actually, this is the most frightening circumstance of all because the student who fails after trying is vulnerable to the threatening conclusion that he lacks ability. Little wonder, then, that many students choose to "fake" their way through rather than to seek out help and thereby make the damaging admission that they do not understand. Of course, this is a total perversion of the purpose of education. These hapless students have confused ignorance with a lack of ability, and as a result they are in danger of remaining ignorant.

In such an atmosphere of exaggeration, success and failure become psychologically remote from one another. We can readily agree with Roger Barker's assessment (1942) that in this situation a miss *is* literally "as good as as a mile" even though the actual difference between a student's expectation and his performance may be quite small, say, the difference of one or two points on a test. Here there is no such thing as a "near miss" nor a sense of progressive improvement toward standards that are possible but not yet attained. In short, one either succeeds or fails. There is no middle ground, no room for the more subtle qualifications of the kind suggested by John Holt (1964) when he urged that schools need to establish a semantic distinction between failure and non-success.

The real tragedy of competition is that it is largely unnecessary. As competitive tendencies increase with age, so does a spirit of cooperation and mutual assistance. Moreover, research also indicates that cooperation can be learned. Once again, we call on Nelson and Kagan (1972). These researchers had some of their young subjects first work together on learning tasks under conditions of sufficient rewards and then later work without enough prizes to go around. For other children this order was reversed. Among the children who practiced cooperation first, there was more willingness to work cooperatively under competitive conditions later on. These students simply split up the small number of prizes on an equal basis after the task was completed. From this and other related research (Masters, 1971), we conclude that cooperation and even altruism can be encouraged so long as students do not always have to compete for insufficient rewards. Again, the key is sufficiency of rewards.

In Summary

The main message of this chapter is that classrooms become failure-oriented because of a scarcity of rewards. Such scarcity is caused largely by a breakdown in self-regulated learning of the kind that has its experimental analogue in the laboratory research of Ferdinand Hoppe. As responsibility for maintaining one's own standards passes out of the hands of individuals, expectations are inevitably driven beyond the reach of many, and the situation is fueled by competitive pressure among students for teacher approval. Tragically, those who are unable to keep pace accuse themselves rather than the inappropriate standards and thereby internalize self-blame and defeat. Few escape this frightening dynamic: by holding himself to unrealistic expectations even the brightest student can suffer the humiliation of failure, while, in reality, his academic record may be outstanding. Perhaps the most troublesome point of all is that teachers are severely limited in their ability to correct this situation. While they may generously reward students for trying hard, in an attempt to offset achievement as the sole source of approval, students, in turn, are prone to judge themselves by the prevailing competitive standards of their peer group. And, as we noted, praise given a student who believes he has done a poor job accomplishes little except perhaps to arouse his suspicions concerning the teacher's motives.

When faced with increasingly stringent expectations, exaggerated values placed on success, and peer hostility, many students abandon their efforts to strive for success and instead take up the burdensome task of trying to avoid failure and the implication that they are worthless. In the next chapter we will document some of the ways students attempt to avoid failure and why it is that they may create the very feelings of shame that they are seeking to escape.

General References

Diggory, J. C. *Self-evaluation: Concepts and studies.* New York: Wiley, 1966.

Holt, J. *How children fail.* New York: Dell, 1964.

Jackson, P. W. *Life in classrooms.* New York: Holt, Rinehart and Winston, 1968.

Purky, W. W. *Self concept and school achievement.* Englewood Cliffs, N.J.: Prentice-Hall, 1970.

Chapter 3 Strategies to Avoid Failure

We have delineated two major kinds of achievement motivation that operate in the classroom: (1) an orientation toward success and (2) a disposition to avoid failure. In this chapter we will examine some of the failure-avoiding tactics used by students as the result of sparse classroom rewards. Generally speaking there are two broad strategies or "game plans" for avoiding failure and its humiliation.

The first of these strategies involves attempts to evade a sense of academic failure when the odds for success are low. This involves disowning the implication that failure holds for one's ability to achieve. The student may arrange things—often through the use of a well-timed excuse or other subterfuge—so that he can blame his failure on something other than low ability and argue, in effect, that failure is no indication of his potential and therefore is not a real measure of his worth. An extreme example of this strategy is the *underachiever,* who by not trying provides no information about his actual ability and consequently experiences little shame when failure overtakes him. Indeed, he may even make a virtue out of his inaction by downgrading the importance of work he refuses to do. Obviously, in the long run such failure-avoiding tactics lead to more rather than fewer failures, and, because of this, they are self-defeating. It is for this reason that we refer to students who repeatedly use such tactics as "failure-prone."

The second set of strategies—quite as ingenious as the first but taking an opposite tack—are attempts to avoid failure and its implications by insuring success. Some of these ploys, such as lowering one's aspirations excessively or cheating in school, are potentially as demoralizing as most failure-prone tactics. Yet there is at least one technique among them, that of *overstriving,* that actually insures a high level of achievement. But we are not to be deceived. Although the compulsive overstriver may have outstanding grades, in reality he is conflicted and anxious because he is motivated to succeed for the wrong reason— as a way to avoid failure.

The first two main sections of Chapter 3 are devoted to a more detailed description and analysis of these two major kinds of failure-avoiding strategies. In third section we will examine some of the factors that predispose the young student, long before he enters school, toward being fearful of failure or hopeful of success.

Failure-prone Strategies

Under this heading we will consider three tactics: nonparticipation, false effort, and irrationally high goal setting. Although each differs, one from the other, in their surface manifestations, they all are employed to the same end—to avoid a *sense* of failure with its implications for ability and feelings of worth.

Nonparticipation. The most direct and obvious of the failure-prone tactics is simply to avoid participation or, to paraphrase the well-known adage, "nothing ventured, nothing failed!" This time-worn ploy is so familiar to every school child as to be a standard feature of classroom life. It takes many forms: slouching down in one's seat to avoid notice by the teacher; appearing eager to answer a question, gambling that the teacher will call on someone else who appears less certain; or busily taking notes, too busy in fact for the teacher to interrupt. These little deceptions are innocuous enough, especially if used sparingly. They serve as a sort of buffer to ease the day-to-day pressures of learning. Nonetheless these tactics are only a few steps away—psychologically speaking—from other more serious manifestations of noninvolvement such as chronic inattention, absenteeism, and dropping out.

Nonparticipation also manifests itself as an unwillingness to do work assignments that are not absolutely required for a grade and in doing as little as possible on required assignments. While research confirms such resistance among failure-prone students (Birney, Burdick, and Teevan, 1969), it is not a tactic that can be repeated with impunity. After all, most schoolwork *is* required, and teachers expect students to participate voluntarily or otherwise. Also, there are strong sanctions against not trying. For this reason nonparticipation as a tactic is usually combined with other more subtle dodges, such as exerting false effort.

False effort. When the fearful student *must* participate, he will do whatever necessary—by hook and sometimes by crook—to sidestep the experience of failure. If he believes striving for success to be too risky a gamble, then one of the best ways to avoid punishment is to exert some degree of effort. This all-purpose strategy is unwittingly set up by the teacher's willingness to reward students "for at least trying." Thus through the simple expediency of appearing to be interested and involved in his schoolwork, a student can enhance the likelihood of praise and, more importantly, escape the extremes of censure. This kind of effort bears little resemblance to the disciplined, spirited effort that is necessary to succeed. Rather we are referring to sham effort: feigning attention during a class discussion; asking a question even though the answer is already known; or giving all the outward appearances of thinking by adopting a pensive, quizzical expression. Basically it is a sham because these students are not trying to succeed, only trying not to fail. Besides, such youngsters have little faith that their efforts—even if they *really* tried—would lead to success.

Obviously, then, students learn more in school than just the three Rs. They also learn to falsify their behavior. And they become enormously inventive at it, sometimes deceiving themselves and their teachers almost indefinitely. But putting this strategy into practice is not as straightforward as might be supposed at first glance. While the student must expend enough energy to escape punishment, he dares not try *too* much. For if he should study hard and still do badly on a particular test, he could no longer blame his failure on a lack of preparation. Instead his ability would come under increased suspicion.

Martin Covington and Carol Omelich (1975) provide evidence on this dilemma—to try, yet not to try—and how students cope with it. These researchers asked college students for their reactions to hypothetical achievement situations in which they were to imagine themselves failing a test that most of their peers had passed. A sense of personal dissatisfaction and public shame was greatest when students studied hard and failed anyway and least when they had not tried at all! This reaction is just the opposite of what one might expect in a society where honest effort counts for something. Effort—even losing effort —should have compensated somewhat for the sting of failure, but it did not. Actually it made things worse. The reason for this curiosity seems clear. These students were interested not so much in the consolation that honest effort brings to a losing cause as they were in avoiding the implication of failure—that they lacked ability. And the best way to avoid this implication is to have an excuse. When these same students were provided with plausible excuses to explain why their effort didn't pay off, their burden of shame and distress decreased sharply. Little wonder then that excuses are such a permanent part of the school scene—students blame tests, arguing that the questions were not the kind one could study for or that the test covered material that they did not emphasize in their study; students shrewdly attack the method of grading as unfair; and sometimes even complain that they were penalized by the cheating of others. Although there may be some truth in each of these allegations, when used repeatedly they are likely to be a form of *rationalization*, a defense mechanism well known to psychologists in which an individual creates false but plausible explanations to justify his behavior. In this case the student is attempting to avoid the personal implications of his poor performance.

The upshot of all this is that these failure-avoiding students can afford neither to do too much nor too little in school. Such students are unwilling to exert effort unless they see their chances of success as reasonably good or unless they can attribute failure to something other than ability. Yet they are obliged to do something. Needless to say, this situation is hardly conducive to the pursuit of personal excellence. In fact, by his actions the student ensures that his performance will be below his potential. Where success is counted only in terms of avoiding failure, personal involvement in real learning is limited, and such a lack of involvement is accompanied inevitably by detachment, apathy, and passivity.

Impossibly high goals. As we have made clear, failure-prone tactics are often employed when the student sees failure as inevitable. Being forced to fail is one of the most demoralizing of all human predicaments. Although the toll it takes is incalculable, the severity of the trauma can at least be imagined through the aid of laboratory research on the conditions that produce irrational behavior. In one kind of experiment animals are forced on pain of severe electric shock to choose between two objects, say, a circle and an ellipse. Selecting the circle always produces a shock equal in intensity to that administered if the animal fails to make a choice, whereas picking the ellipse produces no shock at all. All goes well in the early learning trials. The animal quickly learns to choose the ellipse, and, since the discrimination is an easy one, there is no need to force him to perform. But as the experiment progresses, the ellipse is made to look more and more like the circle until the hapless animal cannot tell them apart. Naturally he now resists making a choice, but he must choose or be punished. Being forced to fail at something over which the animal has no control produces "experimental neurosis" (Cook, 1939). Depending on the species of animals involved, symptoms include loss of appetite, partial paralysis of skeletal muscles, intense agitation alternating with periods of docility, and, on occasion, seizures.

There is an uncomfortable parallel between this diabolical procedure and school learning. Many students know that they cannot avoid failure but are expected to perform anyway—they are damned if they try and damned if they don't! Little wonder that defensive maneuvering in such circumstances takes on an overtone of desperation. Here students may reason that if they cannot avoid actual failure, at least they can try to avoid a *sense* of failure. Ironically, to accomplish this students must set up their own failure.

A common method for setting up such "nonthreatening" failure involves pegging one's aspirations very high—so high, in fact, that success is virtually impossible. To the outside observer such goal setting must seem irrational, but if we view it as a tactic designed to avoid a sense of failure, then it makes perfect sense. Failing an excessively difficult task reveals little about one's capabilities. Moreover, no real blame can be attached to failure when the sought-after goal is beyond the reach of all but the most able.

A shrewd variation on this tactic involves what has been called the "confirming interval" by Robert Birney and his colleagues (1969). This is the psychological interval between the best performance a student expects of himself and the lowest he can attain without experiencing dissatisfaction. Performances that fall within this interval are met with some indifference since they *are* somewhat expected, are acceptable, and do not disconfirm the student's level of aspiration. Naturally by broadening this interval an individual can make subjective failure quite unlikely and with it minimize the painful disconfirmation of self. However, in doing this the student also forfeits real success. In effect, a wide confirming interval can lead to a perpetual state of indifference, where one rarely experiences the shame of failure, but neither does he experience the joys of success. And, as we might predict, failure-avoiding students have been found in several studies to set a far wider confirming interval on tasks where their ability is at stake than do students who are less failure-avoiding (see Birney, Burdick, and Teevan, 1969, pp. 113–25).

By adopting strategies such as these the student progressively cuts himself off from an already scarce supply of classroom rewards. Classroom competition may initially limit the availability of rewards, but using defensive goal setting as a protective device makes a bad situation worse. A perfect example of this is seen in the early pioneer work of Pauline Sears (1940). She discovered that children who had a history of success in their classroom work set their academic goals at a realistic level so that success occurred frequently. In sharp contrast, students who experienced continual frustration and failure in school set *their* aspirations without much regard for present performance levels: they often overestimated—sometimes wildly so—how well they would perform on various arithmetic and reading tasks. For some of these children, the poorer their performance became, the higher they set their aspirations!

This maladaptive behavior is an example of what has been termed "atypical shifts," a phenomenon first noted by Ferdinand Hoppe in his level of aspiration studies where some individuals would raise rather than lower their self-expectations after failure. As Sears (1940, p. 530) points out, this may be caused by an intense, unfulfilled desire for approval in which the mere statement of a worthy goal, and not its attainment, becomes the source of gratification. In effect, the student enters an imaginary realm where fantasies substitute themselves for actual accomplishments.

Underachievers: A Variation on the Theme

The heavy stress placed on classroom achievement coupled with fear of failure produces some dramatic variations in the basic defensive tactics just described. One of the most striking and instructive of these is that of the *under-achiever*. Another, the *overstriver*, will be discussed later. Besides providing a fuller picture of the complexities facing the classroom teacher, the dynamics of the underachiever also shed considerable light on the nature of achievement motivation. Until now we have not considered the various theoretical controversies surrounding this topic. One of the most important of the unresolved issues is whether or not the motive to achieve is a single dimension. The unitary view holds that the dispositions to strive for success and to avoid failure are simply two ends of the same continuum or, to put it differently, two sides of the same coin. Accordingly, all individuals share both these dispositions in common, but in differing proportions; and as one disposition increases in strength, the other is correspondingly reduced. This view is most convincing in the case of individuals who are clearly dominated by one disposition or the other—as we have tended to assume for the sake of simplicity.

The competing view holds that success striving and failure avoidance are two separate dimensions, an arrangement that permits several combinations of student types.

For example, in addition to the individual who is either strongly failure-avoidant or heavily success-oriented, another student might conceivably possess both tendencies in full strength simultaneously. Indeed, many psychologists, in particular Sigmund Freud and his followers, have argued that contradictory tendencies can coexist in the same person. Currently most authorities favor this latter view regarding achievement motivation. The common sense observation seems to have prevailed that persons with a strong need to achieve may also have an intense fear of failure. This is a near-perfect description of underachievers.

Like most adults, teachers believe that it is basically wrong to waste one's natural talents. Consequently, among the most severely punished students are those who have ability but do not use it. Yet despite these severe sanctions many able students use *lack of effort* as a defense against a sense of failure. Not only that, but they also develop a fierce kind of pride in their unwillingness to study. Such a strategy leads to the phenomenon of the underachiever.

The uunderachiever shares with many other students the same unsettling belief that one's entire worth depends on his ability to achieve. But for the underachiever this realization involves more than simply succeeding; it demands academic perfection as well. Most authorities agree that this need for perfection first develops in the early childhood years from the pressure of parents who expect too much too soon (see Bricklin and Bricklin, 1967). Although the data are not yet conclusive, the findings strongly suggest that in their formative years underachievers are rebuked for failing and lauded for their successes, with the net effect that as they grow older these individuals become driven simultaneously to approach success and to avoid failure. But success is in short supply owing to the unrealistically high standards held out by parents and by the fact that these youngsters are given little parental guidance in how best to achieve such idealistic performances (Davids and Hainsworth, 1967). The negative consequences of holding such unforgiving self-standards are illustrated by the distinction between *actual-self* and *ideal-self*. Actual-self refers to how the individual perceives himself to be, while ideal-self is the person as he thinks he *should* be. A number of studies reveal sizeable discrepancies between actual and ideal selves among under-achievers, with the actual-self falling far short of the ideal (see Birney, Burdick, and Teevan, 1969, pp. 145–46). Some psychologists, especially Carl Rogers, have argued that this discrepancy is a measure of mental health with the larger discrepancy appearing in persons who are more disturbed and anxious. Certainly for underachievers this gap produces an almost intolerable situation. They are doomed to disappointment because their idealized self-image is simply beyond their reach in the sense that perfection is beyond the grasp of everyone.

At one level these young students wish they could attain perfection through perfect grades. But the loftiness of this goal increases the pressure, and, they become too anxious to do well. So how can they maintain a sense of worth in the face of poor grades? One answer is to make a virtue— albeit a negative one—out of a poor academic record. Because of his low grades the student becomes unique and different from the majority of his peers (Bricklin and Bricklin, 1967). He comes to take pride in failure as a mark of nonconformity; he may deny the value of hard work and of good grades and is likely to become an outspoken critic of his teacher and school. Of course, this kind of false "individualism" is more to be pitied than admired, originating as it does from a fear of committing oneself to personal effort. By not studying the underachiever neatly avoids any real test of his ability to attain his extraordinarily high aspirations and thus may maintain a defensively inflated opinion of himself. Related to this denial of effort is the belief that he ought to succeed with little or no work. In fact, underachievers are proud of any successes they achieve without much study (Berger, 1961). The implication is that if he had *really* tried, he would have been even *more* successful. There are also secondary advantages to be gained from not trying. The student can punish his parents through his poor academic record, striking at their pride in his previous achievements. In this way he can vent his anger toward them for holding out such high expectations in the first place.

The overwhelming effect of failure-prone tactics is negative and self-defeating. Used in excess—as in the case of the underachiever—they lead to constant failure; and if the student does not experience outright failure, the best he can hope for is a dull, uninspired existence where he cannot win and his only success lies in not losing. In a culture that values achievement and competency there is little payoff for avoiding a sense of failure in this manner.

Insuring Success

Another group of failure-avoiding tactics differs considerably from those just described yet serves the same underlying purpose. These tactics involve insuring success. Under this heading we will consider three different tactics: low goal setting, academic cheating, and overstriving.

Low goal-setting. As we have already discovered, failure-avoiding students prefer difficult tasks and long odds. Likewise, they also prefer easy tasks and for basically the same reason—neither failing a difficult task nor succeeding at an easy one reveals much about one's abilities. And, there is another advantage to always electing the easy job or chronically setting aspirations below one's ability level. It guarantees success of a sort. A typical example is the student who underestimates what he can do by publicly announcing before each test that he will be satisfied with just a "passing" grade. Moreover, as Birney and his colleagues point out (1969, p. 224), there are social payoffs to be gained from such a tactic. Being content with lesser accomplishments can be construed as a form of modesty in which the individual is seen as understating his true potential. At least he cannot be accused of bragging or of not living up to exaggerated claims of excellence.

Yet despite these considerable benefits, chronic low goal-setting is fatally flawed as a defensive device. For one thing, lowering one's standards eventually leads to a deterioration in actual performance (see Locke, 1968). For another, success that is automatically insured becomes cheapened and loses its reward value. Since there is no challenge, there can be no genuine triumph, and students who *do* find satisfaction in such marginal successes have likely entered into the kind of fantasy world that Pauline Sears (1940) described in connection with students who *overestimate* their potential (see p. 49). Here the chronic *under*estimater has engineered an illusory self-respect built on meaningless successes. His defensiveness seems all the more obvious when we recall the tremendous peer pressure on students to keep up with the group and the heavy price students risk for not doing so (for example, social disapproval, even ostracism). To hold out stubbornly for low self-aspirations in the face of such severe sanctions indicates a deep-seated fear of failure.

Academic cheating. Any discussion involving falsification and deception in school inevitably brings to mind the issue of academic cheating. Volumes have been written on this fascinating topic. Some observers, driven by ethical concerns, condemn cheating as one more sign of the widespread moral erosion of our times. In contrast, other investigators search for common underlying pathology among chronic cheaters. Still others view cheating not as evidence of troubled children but as a powerful indictment of an educational system that pressures students into deceit and dishonesty. While each of these perspectives doubtless touches on some part of the truth, we will focus on yet another aspect of the problem—cheating as a tactic to avoid failure. This interpretation of cheating is widely acknowledged among educational psychologists (see Shelton and Hill, 1969). According to this view, cheating should be more prevalent among students of low self-regard than among those who have a high opinion of themselves since failure is more threatening to the former group. It is further argued that high self-esteem discourages dishonesty because it is inconsistent with the prevailing self-image of being worthy and above deception. These hypotheses have been supported in several research studies (see Aronson and Mettee, 1968). There is also evidence of a more personal, poignant kind supplied by students themselves. In one elementary classroom self-confessed cheaters were asked by their teacher to write a brief essay explaining the reasons for their dishonesty. Following are some representative excepts:

Kids don't cheat because they are bad. They are afraid that they aren't smart and what will happen if they don't do good. People will call them dumb or stupid.

If you cheat you will not know how to do the lesson right. You just put off flunking until later. It is scary.

Sometimes teachers don't see cheating. But something terrible will happen to cheaters anyway. They will pay for it. Maybe they will get sick.

I know someone who studies hard for tests and cheats too. They feel really bad but it is better than being yelled at for bad grades.

People cheat because they are afraid of doing poorer than other kids and feeling miserable for being different and behind. Some do it to be the best in class or move to the next group.

One cannot read these revealing confessions without gaining a deeper appreciation of the extent to which the life of the school child is dominated by the fear of failure, of falling behind, of being humiliated. However, like so many other defensive tactics, cheating does not pay. This is not so much because cheating is inherently wrong—as some would have us believe—nor because it robs learning, but rather because, ironically, cheaters come to fear their ill-gotten successes! This occurs because the student knows he is unable to repeat this uncharacteristic performance on his own. Yet he may be expected to do so by his teacher, his parents, or even his peers. In this way the cheater visits retribution upon himself. When such fear of success is combined with a sense of moral guilt for having cheated in the first place, a thoroughly unhealthy situation is created.

Overstriving. As we have already learned, the compulsive overstriver, along with the underachiever, is a prime example of the student who is driven by an intense desire both to succeed and to avoid failure. The basic difference is that while the overstriver is highly successful at avoiding failure through striving, the underachiever has failed in his efforts to attain perfection and therefore has to make a virtue of his unwillingness to learn. Otherwise these two share much in common. Overstrivers are driven by the same devastating belief that plagues the underachiever, that the sole measure of one's worth is his accomplishments. Likewise, both are bedeviled by the same high standards of personal excellence. Here, too, the same pattern of discrepancy between ideal-self and actual-self is found (Martire, 1956). But unlike underachievers, overstrivers are more successful in their attempts to realize their aspirations. They actually *do* get outstanding grades. Indeed, they become almost too successful, for in the long run this success strategy becomes increasingly burdensome. No one can avoid failure indefinitely, despite almost continuous and herculean efforts to do so. We need only recall the research on level of aspiration to realize how frustrating this strategy can be. With each new success comes the necessity of increasing performance in order once again to experience feelings of accomplishment. Thus, it takes progressively greater achievements and more study and preparation to feel worthy. Because success can become such a cruel taskmaster, it is not surprising to find that these seemingly successful students fear success as much as they do failure because it signals yet another escalation of self-demands.

The overstriver accomplishes much through a combination of high ability, overpreparedness, and excessive attention to detail. In fact, it is this emphasis on *effort* that marks the overstriver above all else. But what may be seen as a virtue by the teacher—high achievement through effort—is, ironically, what intensifies the pressure. By relying heavily on effort, the student becomes exceedingly vulnerable in the event of failure. This explains why overstrivers fear failure with a loathing far out of proportion to its importance. Like all failure-avoiding students, the overstriver has fallen victim to a misunderstanding of the proper role of failure in the learning process.

For all these reasons school learning calls out ambivalence and conflict in the overstriver. On the one hand, there is cause for cautious optimism owing to his past history of successful overpreparation. On the other, there is a sense of entrapment because one success demands another, and, of course, there is the ever-present specter of failure.

In Chapter 2 we examined the dynamics of peer-group competition. In doing this we emphasized particularly the plight of those less able pupils who aspire beyond their reach in order to keep up with their more successful fellows. But as we now see, these are not the only victims of a competitive climate. Many of the "pace-setting" students are also victims. Academic success is no guarantee of personal well-being. Indeed, the phenomenon of overstriving serves to deny the widely held, almost sacrosanct belief among educators that, other things being equal, pupils who get the best grades will be the most satisfied with school; and, conversely, that the least successful youngsters will be the most dissatisfied. As a matter of fact, all the available evidence points to there being no relationship at all between success in school and satisfaction with school (Jackson, 1968), despite the well-known fact that rewards tend to arouse positive feelings and punishment, negative feelings.

We are now in a position to understand this apparent contradiction. There is no direct linkage between success and satisfaction because this relationship depends on other factors, chiefly the quality of personal motivation. Students succeed in school for many reasons, not all of them positive—some do it for approval, others out of a competitive impulse, and still others to avoid failure. As a result, successful students are not always satisfied with their school experience or with themselves. The academic overstriver is sufficient proof of this.

Antecedents of Self-regard

What kinds of factors predispose the student toward avoiding failure or toward being hopeful of success? To answer this question we must begin by considering the student as a young child prior to his entering school. We know that children come to school having already had many experiences that have led them to develop certain ideas about their abilities, competency, and worth. It is this self-image, which the child acquires within his family and brings to the classroom, that heavily influences his subsequent achievement patterns. These early self-images serve as blueprints for the kinds of activities the child will undertake, how he expects to be treated by others, and whether he anticipates success or failure in school.

The research in this area points to the overwhelming importance of child-rearing practices and the home environment in influencing the development of childhood self-esteem. Coopersmith (1967, p. 236) has summarized the antecedents of high self-regard in terms of three indispensable parental attitudes and actions: (1) accepting the child in his own right, (2) laying down clear and enforceable rules of conduct, and (3) permitting the child a wide latitude to explore within these boundaries.

Every child must feel approval as a human being; he has the right to expect that any sincere effort on his part will be acceptable. Yet, of course, not all actions are equally acceptable. Definite rules of conduct must be established to help the child learn this vital lesson. Coopersmith (1967, p. 236) indicates several ways in which well-defined limits act to foster self-confidence and a disposition to strive for success. First, firm rules confirm the existence of a social reality that makes demands, dispenses rewards, and punishes infractions. In addition, they strengthen the conviction that it is the child's job to come to understand and master this reality. Through this process of self-mastery the child becomes the agent of his own successes rather than being confused and subjugated by complexities that seem to have neither order nor predictability. Second, clear limits permit the child to gauge accurately his progress toward mastering his environment: he can judge better whether or not he has improved, and, if not, what steps are needed to overcome failure. On the other hand, an absence of standards leaves the child uncertain and less likely to judge himself and his efforts as worthy. Third, clear limits of conduct make for less conflict between parents and children. From all indications, parents who are *authoritative* as opposed to being *authoritarian* are held in greater regard by their children, and the children value themselves more highly. And—most important of all—establishing boundaries does not necessarily restrict the child's freedom of action. In fact, the evidence suggests just the opposite. Families who establish fair but firm rules of conduct tolerate more individual expression than do families without enforceable regulations (Coopersmith, 1967, p. 236). As a result of such freedom to explore, children develop feelings of competency, independence, and a sense of personal responsibility.

Dominating this entire picture of successful child-rearing is a heavy parental emphasis on accomplishment. Parents of high-esteem children expect them to achieve. But while these parents demand much, they also provide the necessary support. This is done mainly through helping the child acquire achievement skills. A clever study by Bernard Rosen and Roy D'Andrade (1959) illustrates this point. These investigators visited the homes of two groups of kindergarten boys, one group identified as high in achievement motivation and the other low. As part of the interview each child was asked to build a tower of irregularly shaped blocks with one hand, while blindfolded. Actually the point of the experiment was to observe the actions of the parents, not the performance of the child. It was found that parents of the high achievement-motivated boys offered more encouragement than did the other parents, mostly in the form of task-oriented hints for solving the problem. Moreover, these parents were more optimistic about how well their sons would do, expected more of them, and expressed more praise and warmth once the task was completed.

An achievement orientation is also reinforced by the way parents react to their child's successes and failures. The evidence suggests that parents of success-oriented children reward performances that come up to their expectations and ignore or remain neutral toward performances that fall short (Teevan and Fischer, 1967). This same tendency has also been found among teachers dealing with success-oriented students. With such consistency from home to school, these patterns are quickly internalized by the student, who comes to praise himself generously for success and to react charitably toward failure (Cook, 1970). In contrast, the parents of failure-avoiding students report the opposite pattern of reinforcement: being noncommittal in response to their children's successes while punishing performances that do not come up to their expectations (Teevan and Fischer, 1967).

On the basis of available research we can reach an important conclusion: the development of self-esteem from within the home depends on a balanced combination of realistic parental expectations, nurturing, task-orientation, and positive reactions to the child's successes and failures.

Of course, many, if not all, of these same qualities are also required of good classroom teachers.

In Summary

We have covered much ground in this chapter. It is now time to draw together the various points we have made into an overview that relates more specifically to the realities of classroom life.

We have seen why it is that each young child enters school already disposed in various ways to protect—or, if need be, to try to salvage—a belief in himself. For self-assured youngsters already confident in their ability to achieve, school simply means another manageable challenge. For other students—most likely the majority—school means striving for success when possible but retreating into defensiveness when necessary. Still other children, already doubtful of their ability to influence events, find the task of protecting their sense of self-worth impossible from the beginning. Needless to say, neither this process of adaptation nor its end result is uniform for all students. Different kinds and combinations of defensive strategies can lead to an almost endless variety of maladaption (e.g., passive indifference, underachieving, and overstriving, to mention just a few). Moreover, there are different degrees of impairment. Some students become thoroughly convinced of their incapacity, while others are left uncertain due to the fact that failure in one academic area is offset by success in another.

Maneuvering to maintain a belief in one's ability to achieve is a far more dynamic process than either laboratory research or casual observation can reflect. In the minute-by-minute reality of classroom life, each student is constantly changing his achievement strategies depending on events. One moment we may find a student trying all out on an assignment—in effect, seizing at success with both hands—because the odds are favorable to him; yet in the next instant his paramount concern is to play it safe, perhaps by waiting for others to answer the teacher's question before committing himself; and still a little later he may hedge his bets in yet another way by bemoaning his lack of preparation for an upcoming test but, in reality, having studied very hard. Such a nonstop performance is worthy of a virtuoso. It is played out largely at an unconscious level with virtually automatic moves and countermoves that depend on the student's intuitive estimates of success and the stakes involved. Moreover, prevailing strategies can change in the time it takes a student to move from one class period to another or from one assignment to another. Yet for all the complexity involved, this drama has but one central purpose—the protection of the individual's sense of worth and dignity.

This analysis portrays students as being somewhat opportunistic and self-serving, albeit for understandable reasons. There is some truth in this. But it is also true that individuals do not act *entirely* like weathervanes, continually shifting their behavior to fit the prevailing conditions of the moment. For one thing, there are powerful forces constantly at work that slowly narrow the student's field of maneuverability and force him into more uniform and less variable achievement patterns: threatened students become more failure-prone or driven to insure success at even greater costs; success-oriented students become more confident and willing to take reasonable risks.

In the next chapter we will consider the nature of the factors that make for an increasing stability of student self-perception. As we shall see, these factors and the processes that they involve depend in large part on the causes to which students (and their teachers) attribute their success and failure.

General References

Birney, R. C., Burdick, H., & Teevan, R. C. *Fear of failure.* New York: Van Nostrand, 1969.

Bricklin, B., & Bricklin, P. M. *Bright child—poor grades.* New York: Dell, 1967.

Coopersmith, S. *The antecedents of self-esteem.* San Francisco and London: Freeman, 1967.

Gilmore, J. V. *The productive personality.* San Francisco: Albion Publishing, 1974.

Horney, K. *The neurotic personality of our time.* New York: Norton, 1937.

Chapter 4 Attributing Causes to Success and Failure

Failure-avoiding tactics are self-defeating—this much is clear from the previous chapter. Their continued use can often lead to disillusionment, mediocrity, and to an overwhelming sense of discouragement. This disheartening process is reflected in the kinds of causes to which failure-avoiding students attribute their successes and failure. Analysis of this type is the province of *attribution theory*. The larger purpose of Chapter 4 is to integrate the findings of attribution theory with our previous insights into the dynamics of fear of failure. This will lead us to explanations for several student behaviors that have long puzzled and often exasperated teachers—why students sometimes reject their own successes, why failure motivates some students but inhibits others, and why many students are afraid to try hard in school.

Some Paradoxes

One might assume at first glance that failure-avoiding tactics could be reversed by providing students with their fair share of successes. It makes sense, after all, that if a scarcity of success experiences is the original culprit, then providing compensatory rewards should set things right. Moreover, according to reinforcement theory, individuals ought to seek out success once they find how satisfying it can be. Yet, despite this logic, things do not always work out this way. Failure-avoiding students are largely unresponsive to success, something teachers know only too well. Indeed, such pupils seem almost calculating in their disregard for the success experiences that teachers carefully set up for them. Another puzzling observation is that failure, far from discouraging success-oriented students, actually appears to motivate them to greater effort! This also runs counter to a strict reinforcement view of learning, which predicts that failure ought to inhibit achievement. These apparent paradoxes are resolved when we realize that there are other important factors in learning beyond the sheer frequency and strength of rewards and punishments. There are also the person's beliefs about what *cause* his successes and failures. As is often true in psychology, the way a person perceives an event can be as important as the fact that it occurred in the first place.

Attribution Theory

Once a student sees himself as a failure, the meaning of success changes so that it no longer holds much reward value for him. Success becomes an unexpected event, and therefore it is likely to be attributed by the student to causes outside himself such as the ease of the task or good luck. Success that is "bestowed by fate" does little to increase a person's sense of confidence, no matter how often it occurs. This kind of analysis is an example of attribution theory.

Attribution theory as it applies to achievement behavior is the study of the kinds of explanations people give for their successes and failures and the consequences of their doing so. Actually we have been using attribution theory and its terms at an intuitive, commonsense level throughout this book. Now by understanding something of the formal properties of this theory, we can gain additional insights into the dynamics of school achievement, confidence, and a sense of self-worth.

In the late 1950s the groundwork for an attribution model of achievement motivation was laid by Fritz Heider in his brilliant essay on human motivation (1958). During the following decade, Heider's inspired armchair speculations were refined and formalized, first by Julian Rotter (1966) and more recently by Bernard Weiner and his colleagues (1971). These efforts have led to an enormous number of studies that seek to test Heider's original notions and extend them in a number of exciting directions.

In its most contemporary form, attribution theory proposes that four different kinds of explanations are used by individuals to account for their performance in achievement situations. These already familiar elements are: (1) ability, (2) effort, (3) task difficulty, and (4) chance or luck. This last category includes a number of miscellaneous and capricious factors such as fatigue, temporary mood, and teacher bias.

These elements and their interaction can be described in a number of ways. The discussion that follows is based on the approach of Bernard Weiner (1971, p. 96). The first two of these elements (ability and effort) refer to qualities of the *person* while the other two components (task difficulty and luck) are properties of the *environment*. Moreover, two of these components (ability and task difficulty) are stable in nature, whereas the others (luck and effort) are subject to constant change. Thus, these four components can be arranged along two dimensions. The first of these is an internal versus external dimension or, as it is frequently called, *locus of control*. This simply refers to whether a person's achievements are seen as being under his own control (determined by forces within himself, such as ability or effort) or are seen as being caused by forces external to the person (task difficulty and luck). The other dimension refers to the degree of stability of factors contributing to achievement, either stable or unstable. This entire analysis can be summarized in tabular form and is presented in Table 4.1.

Table 4.1
Classification Scheme for the Perceived
Determinants of Achievement Behavior

Stability	*Locus of Control*	
	Internal	External
Stable	Ability	Task difficulty
Unstable	Effort	Luck

From Weiner B., Frieze, I., Kukla, A., Reed, L., Rest, S., & Rosenbaum, R. Perceiving the causes of success and failure. In E. E. Jones (Ed.), *Attribution: Perceiving the causes of behavior.* New York: General Learning Press, 1971, p. 96. Copyright 1971, Silver Burdett Company/General Learning Press. Reprinted by permission.

Under what conditions do individuals assign these four causes to their performance, and how do these explanations affect subsequent achievement? These complex questions are best answered through example.

First, take the matter of assigning causes to one's performance. Consider a student who has just received a high score on, say, a spelling test. He is likely to attribute his success to superior ability to the extent that he has always done well in spelling, studied very little for this particular test (low effort), and noticed that few other students got as good a score as he did (high task difficulty). In contrast, another student who did equally well might attribute his success entirely to lucky guessing if he had never done well before and had studied only indifferently for this test. Of course, there are as many conclusions possible as there are students taking the test, with each interpretation depending on the particular pupil's history of past success and failure, on his test score, and so on.

Now consider what effects such attributions have on the quality of future performance. Take the first student again. In his case success will likely act to increase confidence since he attributed it to his own skill. For the second student, however, the impact of success will be negligible since he takes no credit for it. Likewise, in the event of failure, attributions affect future expectations in a similar way. A person who failed the spelling test but attributed that failure to a lack of effort will likely maintain a hope for the future and will probably try even harder next time, but the person who sees his failure as being due to a lack of ability will likely despair of ever doing better. With this brief background in mind we can now consider the attribution patterns found among success-oriented and failure-avoiding students.

Attributions among Success-oriented Students

Repeated success is taken as evidence of sufficient ability —if a person did well on previous occasions, presumably he has the capacity to do well again. Since success-oriented students are frequently successful, they naturally come to see themselves as equal to most academic demands. With their ability no longer at issue, these students view success and failure as being largely dependent on the quality of their effort. Indeed, the research evidence is remarkably consistent on this point—success-oriented students tend to attribute success to *ability* and *effort* and failure to a *lack* of proper effort (see Weiner and Kukla, 1970). Clearly this interpretation is positive and uplifting. In effect, success inspires further confidence because it is taken as evidence of one's ability to do well, while failure signals the need to try harder. Also, such an interpretation robs failure of its threat! Failure does not necessarily reflect on one's ability; furthermore it can usually be set right by a redoubling of effort. This explains one of our paradoxes— why failure can act to motivate the already successful student. Moreover, since their ability to do well is not in question, these youngsters are more able to accept their limits and work within them, even in the face of occasional failures. A case in point is their preference for moderate risk taking. This means setting goals high enough so that there is some chance of failure but not so high that success is unlikely. Such a strategy gives the individual considerable information about his capabilities. For example, failing to reach a challenging but not impossible goal tells the individual far more about his strengths and weaknesses than if he had failed at an impossibly difficult task or succeeded at a very simple one. Success-oriented students use this information to make intelligent decisions about where and when to compete for rewards, a practice that increases the likelihood of future success.

In sum, success-oriented students take charge of their own achievements. Their locus of control is internal—they believe themselves to be the cause of their successes and accept personal responsibility for their failures. To use the colorful distinction proposed by Richard de Charms (1968), these students are *Origins*—that is, in personal control of events—as contrasted to youngsters who see themselves as *Pawns*—helpless in the hands of powerful others. Individuals who are confident that they control their own destiny are more likely to succeed because they value learning more, work harder, and expect to be successful (Battle and Rotter, 1963; Omelich, 1974b). They also remain realistic in their judgments despite peer pressure to conform (Odell, 1959), and they react constructively to frustration and failure (Butterfield, 1964).

The result of these dynamics is an upward spiraling of achievement and enhanced confidence. However, we are not suggesting that this buoyant process is a closed system incapable of being reversed. Far from it. In fact, John

Flowers (1974) has demonstrated just how vulnerable the process is. Flowers administered a math test to groups of fourth grade students who were matched on quantitative ability. One group was told to praise themselves whenever they finished a problem that they were sure they had answered correctly. A second group was instructed to criticize themselves whenever they were unsure of an answer. As a result of this self-induced doubt, the test performances of the second group deteriorated badly, while the scores of the first group actually increased. Obviously worry interferes with performance, but what is even more distressing is the ease with which academic performance can be undermined, especially among students who were reasonably confident to begin with. Had the doubt been genuine and not artificially induced, the consequences of poor performance might have been disastrous for some of these children. The seeds of self-doubt can be sown so easily and in so many different ways. This fact makes the pursuit of personal excellence an uncertain affair.

Attributions among Failure-avoiding Students

If the road to personal excellence is rocky and filled with surprises, the downside of this dynamic is at least more predictable. Here events can be traced with far greater certainty. This dubious advantage arises out of the grim, relentless forces that conspire against students to create self-doubt, frustration, and a sense of hopelessness. Failure-prone students feel impotent and powerless in school. They tend to attribute their failures to a lack of ability and ascribe their successes—infrequent as they may be—to external factors such as the momentary generosity of the teacher, lucky guessing, or an easy task (Weiner and Kukla, 1970). It is difficult to imagine a more calamitous pattern of attributions—the student blames himself for failure, yet takes little or no credit for his successes. Feeling at the mercy of capricious forces beyond one's control is demoralizing, especially in an academic context where failure threatens self-respect. The student has little choice but to minimize pain by trying to avoid failure. Yet it is this defensiveness, coupled with increasing anxiety and self-defeating attributions, that literally guarantees his failure. This bleak situation is made worse by the conviction that nothing positive can be done.

The phenomenon of "learned helplessness" provides a dramatic demonstration of the effects of feeling powerless. Seligman, Maier, and Geer (1968) subjected dogs to intensive electric shocks from which there was no escape despite all their frantic efforts. Later the experimental conditions were altered so the animals could easily avoid the shock by learning a simple escape response, something that would take only one or two trials under normal circumstances. Yet many of the punished dogs never did learn. They had learned to be helpless due to their prior experience that had demonstrated they had no control over events.

Failure-prone children are victimized by many of the same dynamics (Dweck and Reppucci, 1973). The most self-destructive of them become helpless because in their experience it seems not to matter how hard they try, the outcome is nearly always the same—failure. Of course, their failures, in fact, have less to do with the amount of effort expended than with its quality. Anxiety undercuts the best intentions of these students, causing a blind, mechanical persistence rather than a flexible, adaptive pursuit of the task. Moreover, failure-prone tactics cause the student to squander his efforts in meaningless ways. Thus, these students come to blame their failures on insufficient ability. Indeed, their experiences literally compel this conclusion. "Since trying did not help, then my problem must be low ability, . . . so why try"? As erroneous as such conclusions are, they make sense to the student because they are consistent with his growing image of himself as a failure. For these reasons, such beliefs are extraordinarily difficult to combat.

Under the circumstances blaming one's failure on insufficient ability is quite understandable. But what is puzzling, even paradoxical, is the tendency to reject success—paradoxical, because it is done despite the overriding human need to enhance and protect a sense of self-worth. This paradox is resolved by recognizing the fact that there exist strong countervailing reasons for denying one's successes. These reasons can be understood in attributional terms. Success implies an obligation to do well again; indeed, both parents and teachers believe that one success deserves another. But the low-esteem student cannot live up to the promise of his high achievement, believing as he does that success is not of his own making. The situation is somewhat analogous to the successful cheater who finds himself in the awkward position of being unable to repeat his ill-gotten success on his own. Add to this the strong tendency among individuals to maintain a consistent and stable self-image (see Jones, 1973)—even a negative one—and we have a powerful mechanism for perpetuating denial of success.

As failure becomes an accepted way of life, the prospects for changing things grow dim. The extent of the difficulties involved in reversing this trend is illustrated by a sobering research finding. Not only do failure-prone individuals tend to deny success once it occurs, but they frequently act counterproductively to keep success from occurring at all (Aronson and Carlsmith, 1962). In effect, these individuals sabotage their own efforts when they find themselves in danger of succeeding!

Incidentally, data have recently come to light that suggest the existence of yet another kind of success-avoidance, differing greatly in purpose, and limited to women and girls. Matina Horner (1972) has shown that teen-age girls deliberately hold back their achievements when placed in competition with males for fear of being rejected socially and of feeling unfeminine should they succeed. This kind of inhibition is not to be confused with a fear of being *unable* to succeed—these girls were confident enough—but rather it is the prohibition of an otherwise healthy desire to achieve. This finding suggests that in our society girls and women are placed in "double jeopardy" when it comes to pursuing success. Even if a young woman manages to avoid fear of failure and develops a strong achievement orientation, success still may be denied her because it is at odds with the dominant stereotype of women as non-achievers.

So far, then, the implication is that two antagonistic tendencies come into play whenever chronic low-esteem students, either male or female, have an unexpected success: a natural desire to accept success and a competing need to reject it for fear of the obligation it creates. Sometimes the self-aggrandizing value of success is the more powerful; at other times, a need to avoid obligations at all costs seems to dominate. It is enormously important that we understand something of the factors that influence the relative strengths of these opposing tendencies. For until the low-esteem student can accept his own successes, there is little hope of enhancing confidence in his ability.

Investigators have discovered at least two factors that affect this balance. The first has to do with the already familiar matter of *obligation*: individuals of low self-esteem tend to reject success if they believe they will later be obliged to repeat it (Jones, 1973; Mettee, 1971). An extreme example of this is the unfortunate student for whom success is acceptable only if it is seen as occurring through chance or as a lucky break. The second factor involves the matter of *certainty*, the degree to which the individual is certain about the accuracy of his self-appraisal. Students who are completely convinced of their impotency tend to reject success, whereas those who are still uncertain of themselves, embrace it. This point is illustrated by the research of Stanley Coopersmith (1967). Coopersmith identified two differing types of low-esteem boys. One type not only doubted themselves but were also held in low regard by their peers and teachers. It has been proposed (see Marecek and Mettee, 1972) that these boys were quite *certain* about the validity of their negative self-appraisal owing to the fact that others confirmed it, and, as a consequence, they became trapped in a self-image of failure. In effect, they had abandoned efforts to maintain a sense of worth. The other boys were also low in self-esteem but by contrast were held in *high* regard by their peers and teachers. These youngsters were far more successful in school, again according to speculation, because they were *less* certain about their true potential and sought to reduce this uncertainty by striving to prove their worth both to themselves and others. It is quite possible that these children are well on their way to becoming what we have described as *overstrivers*, where one's value must be proven constantly through an unbroken string of successes.

An ingenious experiment by Jeanne Marecek and David Mettee (1972) examined the joint effect on performance of these two factors, obligation and certainty of self-appraisal. College women were divided into two groups, one high and the other low in self-esteem. The two groups were then further divided according to degree of certainty about their self-appraisals, either high or low certainty. These four groups were given a task that required perceptual speed and accuracy. Half the students were told that performance depended on intellectual ability (skill condition). The others were told that it was all a matter of chance (luck condition). Halfway through their work on the task, all groups were given bogus norms purporting to represent the performance of typical college students. Since these fake norms were deliberately low, all students were confronted with highly successful performances. The crux of this experiment is what happened to the subsequent performance of low-esteem students in the face of such unexpected success. But first a word about the two high-esteem groups. These students uniformly increased their performance on the second half of the task, regardless of whether they were certain or uncertain about their self-appraisal or whether they worked under conditions of luck or skill. As we have seen, success has a powerful motivating effect on the performance of already successful individuals.

Now what of the reaction of the low-esteem individuals to success? First, consider the low-esteem/uncertain students. Their performance increased under both luck and skill conditions. They embraced success, and their subsequent performance was thereby increased. This lends weight to our earlier claim (see p. 74) that students who have not yet completely internalized their past failures may still be able to accept their own praiseworthy achievements. However, the data for low-esteem/certain students is far less optimistic. Under the skill conditions, the performance of this group fell sharply. Since their performance on the first half of the task was the same as for all other groups, this sudden decrease cannot be easily explained away by insufficient ability, boredom, or a sense of discouragement. Rather, we see here a prime instance of students unwittingly suppressing their own performance to compensate for an unexpected success. In short, these individuals could not handle success and the obligation it implies. On the other hand, success *can* motivate these students as long as it is seen as a windfall or a lucky break. Under the luck condition these low-esteem/certain students actually increased their performance, in fact, by enough to surpass the performances of the other three groups! Of course, this kind of increase is not very reassuring. If the only time a student can perform in a superior manner is when he is convinced that his successes have nothing to do with his own effort and he feels no obligations, then the pursuit of excellence is made impossible.

Despite the pessimistic implications, this and other similar experiments (Pepitone *et al.*, 1969) suggest some important guidelines to the teacher. For one thing, they illustrate the crucial importance of intervening as early as possible before failure becomes a chronic way of life. As long as a student is somewhat uncertain about the causes of his failures, he may respond well to praise and success. For another thing, they underscore the importance of not treating all low-esteem students alike.

Teachers and the Self-fulfilling Prophecy

Not only do students attribute causes to their behavior but so do their teachers, and teacher attributions in turn play a vital part in determining the achievement level of students. As only one example (one we have used before), pupils who are perceived by teachers as expending energy are praised more and punished less than those who do not try (Lanzetta and Hannah, 1969). Likewise, the most severely punished students are those who have ability but do not study, as if it were immoral to waste one's natural talents. The consequences of this interaction between teacher and student attributions is illustrated by the example of a young student named Sandra.

In recent months Sandra has been doing poorly in school. None too confident to begin with, Sandra attributes these setbacks with increasing certainty to a lack of ability. As this conviction grows, so does Sandra's despair, until finally she gives up trying at all. By now even her occasional successes and any accompanying teacher praise are shrugged off as unimportant. Meanwhile, the teacher interprets "no effort" as a sign of laziness, and since praise does not seem to work, he censures Sandra in a last-ditch effort to motivate her. When this fails, he lowers his expectations and, in effect, begins to give up on Sandra, too.

Such changes in teacher expectation are conveyed to students partly through the mechanism of reward and punishment mentioned above but also in a number of other ways. For example, it is known that teachers spend less time with students for whom they have low expectations (Felsenthal, 1970). But, not only does the amount of time spent differ, the quality of the relationship differs as well. According to Goldenberg (1969), teachers tend to work with their best students during the time of day when they and their students are freshest. Moreover, Rowe (1972) notes a tendency among primary school teachers to wait longer for high ability students to answer their questions and to supply answers impatiently to children of lesser ability, thus depriving these latter youngsters of the opportunity to learn to think through and formulate their own ideas.

These are only a few of the many ways that teachers express their expectations toward students in the form of concrete behavior. Naturally these actions affect the quality of student performance and ultimately self-confidence (see Meichenbaum and Bowers, 1969). In Sandra's case they served to discourage further effort on her part, which depresses her performance even more. To Sandra this is convincing proof that she is indeed a failure, something both she and her teacher may have suspected all along.

Sandra's plight illustrates the twin concepts of *teacher expectation* and *self-fulfilling prophecy*. Teachers anticipate that certain pupils will succeed in school, while others will not. These expectations invariably affect the way teachers relate to students, and the student in turn reflects these expectations through his own actions so that in time he comes to fulfill the teacher's original prophecy. When teacher expectations challenge students to achieve at their best, a reciprocal process is set in motion that is at once expansive and exhilarating for students. However, if a teacher's expectations undermine rather than challenge the student, the reciprocal process can be a brutalizing experience.

A frightening example of how this process can shape the destiny of an entire classroom is provided by Ray Rist (1970), who followed the fortunes of a group of ghetto children through the first three years of school. After the first eight days of school, the kindergarten teacher identified the "fast" and "slow" learners in the group and assigned them to different work tables. Rist convincingly demonstrates that these placements were made not so much on the grounds of academic potential—no test scores were available to the teacher—but, in reality, according to social class differences within the group. Children who best fit the teacher's middle-class "ideal" (e.g., neat appearance, courteous manner, and a facility with Standard American English) were seated at Table 1, while everybody else was relegated to an inferior status. Predictably the teacher spent the majority of her time and energy on the students at Table 1. Just as predictably, this led to a lack of interest and restlessness at Tables 2 and 3, so that when the teacher *did* attend to these students, it usually took the form of reprimands for misconduct ("sit down"). From the lack of attention and teaching, these students made little or no progress, which further convinced the teacher of the correctness of her original judgment that these were indeed nonlearners. Sensing the teacher's low regard for these children, the students at Table 1 began to ridicule them ("I'm smarter than you"; "The answer is easy, stupid"). The youngsters at Tables 2 and 3 reacted by withdrawal, self-blame, and hostility directed within their own group. In effect, these children were internalizing what the students at Table 1 were saying about them.

The label of "fast" and "slow" learner was reinforced throughout the kindergarten year, first by the teacher and then by the students themselves, so that when it came time for first grade, these labels, which were originally informal, took on an official character in the form of cumulative records. Acting on these evaluations, the first grade teacher assigned the children to *new* reading groups but in predictable ways. No child who had sat at Tables 2 or 3 in kindergarten was placed in the top group; conversely, with the exception of one student, no one from Table 1 was placed in the middle or low reading groups. Later, when these same students entered second grade, the names of the reading groups changed once again, but the pattern of placement remained virtually the same. Summarizing his three years of observation, Rist (1970) laments:

No matter how well a child in the lower reading groups might have read, he was destined to remain in the same reading group. This is, in a sense, another manifestation of the self-fulfilling prophecy in that a "slow learner" had no option but to continue to be a slow learner, regardless of performance or potential. . . . The child's journey through the early grades of school at one reading level and in one social grouping appeared to be pre-ordained from the eighth day of kindergarten [p. 435].

At the heart of this self-fulfilling process are the causes to which teachers attribute student performance. It is these attributions that largely determine whether a student's performance will be praised or punished and how much. These relationships are clearly demonstrated in a series of recent research studies conducted by Bernard Weiner and his colleagues (see Weiner and Kukla, 1970). In a typical study student teachers were given information about a number of hypothetical students. These facts included how well the student did on a test (either excellent, fair, borderline, moderate failure, or clear failure), the student's ability level (either high or low), and the degree of effort expended in studying for the test (either high or low). The teachers then provided feedback to each hypothetical student in light of his test performance. Rewards were conveyed in the form of gold stars and could be varied from one to ten stars depending on how much praise the teacher felt the student deserved. Punishment was in the form of red stars and could be varied in the same way. Each teacher evaluated all hypothetical pupil combinations, such as a high ability student who did not expend effort and clearly failed, and so forth. The results of one representative study using student teachers (Weiner and Kukla, 1970) are presented in Figure 4.1.

These findings confirm much of what we have already discovered about the burden of conflicting pressures on teachers regarding the encouragement of student performance. First of all, there is unmistakable evidence that teachers strongly reinforce *achievement* as the *primary* classroom value. Irrespective of the personal characteristics of students—whether they are able or not, motivated or unmotivated, or some combination of these factors—teach-

Figure 4.1
Evaluation (reward and punishment) as a function
of pupil ability, motivation, and examination outcome

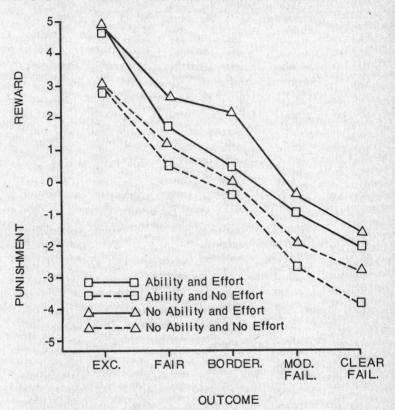

Adapted from Weiner, B., and Kukla, A. An attributional analysis
of achievement motivation. *Journal of Personality and Social Psychology,* 1970, 15(1), 1–20. Copyright 1970 by the American Psychological Association. Reprinted by permission.

ers still tend to reward good performance and to punish
failure. Yet while achievement is the overriding index of
merit, it is not conclusive. Within limits, teachers do manage to reinforce a "work ethic." This tendency is also illustrated in Figure 4.1 by the fact that some students are
rewarded (or punished) more than others for exactly the

same level of performance. Here the degree of reward or punishment depends on the perceived causes of the student's performance, and by far the most important of these factors is student effort. Students who are perceived as having expended effort (regardless of their ability level) are rewarded more and punished less than pupils who did not try. The importance of perceived effort is best illustrated in Figure 4.1 by the group of hypothetical students with low ability who tried. This group is evaluated more favorably than any other, even beyond the high ability students who also tried! Here the teacher is acting as a conveyer of the cultural norm. He is being democratic; not everyone has high ability, but everyone *can* try, and such effort should be rewarded. By being willing to reward effort the teacher reveals far more understanding about the pursuit of excellence than some critics are willing to concede. However, before we flatter the teacher unduly we must remember that *achievement* is still the dominant classroom virtue—success is valued more than failure no matter how well-intentioned or motivated the failing student might be. Moreover, the effects of rewarding effort differ for various kinds of students, and they are not all positive.

First, take the success-oriented student. Here the teacher's emphasis on effort reinforces striving for success and the attributions that sustain it. High accomplishment among able students who try hard is generously rewarded, as seen in Figure 4.1. This reinforces student confidence and a willingness to try again. On the other hand, when the successful student fails, his ability is not questioned because of his prevailing successes. Rather, failure is attributed to lack of effort and hence is punishable by the teacher to varying degrees depending on its severity. Rarely, however, is the performance of these students poor enough to warrant severe criticism. Moreover, other research indicates that, if anything, teachers tend to ignore the occasional failures of able students who usually work hard (Rest *et al.*, 1973). It will be recalled that this teacher pattern of recognition for success and forbearance in the event of failure is identical to the child-rearing practices that reinforce high achievement motivation in the home (Teevan and Fischer, 1967).

Next, consider failure-avoiding students. Here the interaction between teacher and student takes a decidedly less healthy turn. We know from Figure 4.1 that in the event of failure the students punished most are those who do not try. But, as we also learned in Chapter 3, failure holds less personal threat for students when they do not exert much effort. With the juxtaposing of these two findings, the irony is complete. Students prefer to set themselves up for precisely what teachers punish most—noneffort. Realistically, of course, students must try to some degree, even if it is only false effort. By the self-serving tactic of appearing interested and involved in his school work a student can escape the extremes of censure no matter how poorly he performs. In fact, it is quite amazing just how little reprimand is given students who fail, even outrageously, as long as they are perceived as having tried. Figure 4.1 illustrates just how handsomely this deception can pay off.

The net result is that the failure-avoiding student must thread his way between the threatening extremes of high effort and no effort at all. He must exert some effort to avoid teacher punishment but not so much as to risk public shame should he fail. Excuses are his chief ally in maintaining this precarious balance. First, consider the danger of too much effort. We have already seen in Chapter 3 how excuses protect the student against a demotion of his ability in the eyes of peers should he try hard and still fail. We are all familiar with the student who confides to his friends that the test covered material he did not study. Now what of the threat of too little effort? Here, too, excuses are quite effective. Just how effective is demonstrated in recent research by Martin Covington and Carol Omelich (1975). These researchers repeated the study presented in Figure 4.1 but with one additional piece of information about each hypothetical student—whether or not he had an excuse. From these data it appears that teachers make allowances for low effort even in failure *if* the student has a plausible explanation for why he did not study; otherwise he is severely censured.

Thus there emerges from this complex interplay among students, peers, and teacher a "winning" formula in the anticipation of failure that is designed to avoid personal humiliation and shame on the one hand and to minimize teacher punishment on the other: try, or at least *appear* to try, but not too energetically and with excuses handy. It is difficult to imagine a strategy better calculated to sabotage the pursuit of personal excellence.

Distressing as this is, there is even worse to come. According to Figure 4.1, the most brutalizing effect of teacher evaluation is reserved for the underachiever. Since these students are known to have sufficient ability, the cause of their failure is naturally attributed to a lack of effort. Consequently, this group (ability/no effort) is the most severely punished for failure of all the groups. However, since underachievement serves a defensive purpose, the student is unlikely to change his ways in response to punishment, coercion, or threat. In fact, such treatment is likely to increase resistance, not reduce it. Thus the student is condemned to endure a continual barrage of punishment. By referring to Figure 4.1 once again, we can complete our understanding of this particular cycle of self-discouragement. Even on those infrequent occasions when underachieving students do well, they are the least rewarded of all the groups. Excessive disapproval for failure and faint praise for success is a damning formula. Little wonder that underachievers are filled with resentment and hostility toward both themselves and others.

In Summary

Our account of the nature of the threat to self-worth, its causes, and consequences is now complete. From the perspective built up over the four preceding chapters we can integrate a number of themes into a meaningful and comprehensive picture. This analysis takes us to the very heart of the cycle of self-discouragement, which often grips teacher and student alike.

At bottom everything reduces to a fundamental conflict of objectives. Most simply put, teachers and students often operate at cross-purposes in the classroom. Above all, teachers value high achievement. Indeed, they are hired to ensure competency, and in the process they praise effort as a motivating device and because it seems fair. Yet for the failure-prone student, expending effort represents a personal threat. If he should study hard and still fail, his ability to achieve is thrown into question. The objective of these students, then, is quite different from that of the teacher. Above all, they are attempting to protect self-worth, in effect, to shun the implication that they lack the ability to achieve in an achievement-oriented society. Consequently, such students are often reluctant to participate and fear to ask questions that might reveal their ignorance. And if they do make themselves vulnerable in these ways, they manage to have excuses handy to evade the implications of failure should it occur. A mixture of excuses, false effort, and subterfuge seems the best strategy under the circumstances. It is this student behavior that so frustrates the conscientious teacher.

Many misunderstandings occur when teacher and student values are at odds. For example, take the matter of laziness. Much of what passes for laziness is an effort by students to aggrandize their ability. The most conclusive proof of one's brilliance is to study as little as possible and still do well. (This practice has the added advantage of serving as an excuse if the student does poorly!) Disapproving of low effort as they do, teachers are likely to pronounce the student lazy and unmotivated. But the student is far from unmotivated. To the contrary, he is highly motivated but for the wrong reasons. He is trying hard to avoid failure and to protect his sense of worth.

From this already dismal reconstruction of classroom dynamics we draw another sobering conclusion. It is widely believed—indeed, virtually an article of faith among many teachers—that student effort can be controlled through the judicious use of praise, chiding, coaxing, and even ridicule. But, as we now know, this belief is largely false. The teacher's ability to promote student effort is severely limited. The exception to this is the success-oriented pupil who responds to teacher reprimand with increased effort and to praise with renewed striving. This harmonious situation is due to the fact that these students, their teachers, *and* their parents all share an abiding belief in the value of individual achievement and a conviction that personal *effort* is the key to success. Here there is no conflict of values; students and teachers are motivated to the same ends.

The situation is, of course, markedly different for the failure-avoiding student. Using punishment as a motivating device here is no good at all. Indeed, it only makes matters worse by acting as additional confirmation of his failure and may lead the student to further inaction or drive him to defensive maneuvering on an even more exaggerated scale. Either way, the outcome is the same: a reduction in productive, self-confident behavior. Teacher praise as a strategy fares little better. Praise is discounted by the chronic avoider because he perceives his praise-worthy behavior as being caused by external forces. The effectiveness of praise is further eroded when it is unwittingly dispensed for behaviors that the student regards as failures. And, above all, praise is shunned whenever the student feels the obligation to repeat his successes on some future occasion.

In the opening pages of his book, we likened this interplay between teacher and student to a kind of modern Greek tragedy in which, despite the best intentions of everyone, students are wasted and teachers become disillusioned. We now add to this already alarming analysis an additional note of apprehension—that teachers are largely powerless to correct the situation, at least as long as the learning structure remains failure-oriented. The burden of the second half of this book is to explore ways to remedy the problem. The key to this, as we shall see, is to change the yardstick by which students measure their successes and failures, a transformation that involves restructuring the rules of the learning game. It is to this task that we now turn.

General References

LaBenne, W. D., & Greene, B. I. *Educational implications of self-concept theory*. Pacific Palisades, Cal.: Goodyear Publishing Co., 1969.

Rist, R. C. Student social class and teacher expectations: The self-fulfilling prophecy in ghetto education. *Harvard Educational Review*, 1970, **40**, 411–50.

Rosenthal, R., & Jacobson, L. *Pygmalion in the Classroom*. New York: Holt, Rinehart and Winston, 1968.

Strom, R. D., & Torrance, E. P. *Education for affective achievement*. New York: Rand McNally & Co., 1973.

Weiner, B. Attribution theory, achievement motivation, and the educational process. *Review of educational research*, 1972, **42**, 203–15.

Chapter 5 Success-oriented Learning Structures

In the four preceding chapters we have examined the dynamics of fear of failure and the complex relationships that exist among academic achievement, confidence, and feelings of self-worth. In the remaining chapters we will consider what can be done to reduce the threat of failure and, in the process, to strengthen a will to learn among students. But before proceeding, we must understand clearly what the problem is and what its probable causes are.

A Brief Review

In our society young people quickly learn to assume that their worth as human beings depends heavily on the ability to achieve. This belief is first laid down in the home and then hardened to conviction in the schools. It is for this reason that learning becomes a potential threat, for should the student fail to achieve or to live up to the expectations of others, he risks rejection and loss of esteem. All too often classrooms produce more feelings of failure than of success owing chiefly to knife-edge competition, a lack of clarity of learning goals, and a misunderstanding of the proper role of failure in learning. Consequently, many students see themselves as unable to compete successfully for a fair share of the available rewards, so instead they try to protect themselves by maneuvering to avoid failure or a sense of failure at not having reached "the top." And, it is these defensive strategies that produce apathy, mediocrity, and sometimes, ironically, failure itself. The root problem then is that in our society worth is gauged largely by competitive achievement. This poses a threat to those who are doubtful of their ability to achieve in competitive situations.

Now consider the matter of solutions. Some observers have been confused on this point and have suggested cures for the wrong problem. There have always been those who believe that treating everyone alike—in effect, suppressing individual differences in achievement and creating a near uniformity—will produce a shared sense of equal dignity. Proponents of this strategy, which John Gardner (1961) characterizes as "equalitarianism wrongly conceived [p. 15]" do not appreciate that a sense of worth and dignity is achieved largely through striving toward individual excellence. Bringing the achievement of all to the same level will only result in mediocrity and in the process will destroy the spirit of individual initiative so crucial to high accomplishment. A contemporary variation on this equalitarian strategy is the suggestion that teachers should instruct in such a way that no students experience failure. This position assumes that failure *per se* causes loss of esteem and self-respect. Of course, this is *not* necessarily true. As we have seen repeatedly, failure can act as an important factor in motivating achievement as long as the failure is interpreted properly and does not become a way of life. In any event, to shield students from failure experiences is no kindness; it prepares them for a world that does not exist.

We cannot enhance self-worth, nor can we foster high accomplishment by ignoring individual differences in talent and ability. Actually, we must encourage rather than discourage different kinds of excellence, yet at the same time—and this is the important point—we must make certain that the resulting diversity does not unduly threaten the individual.

Elements of a Solution

The nub of the difficulty is that in schools the payoff comes from successful performance. But this kind of success typically is measured in terms of how much better one person did than someone else. In short, students can maintain their sense of self-worth only by making others feel unworthy! This situation produces a tangled skein of causes, effects, and negative consequences that resembles the legendary Gordian knot. Unlike the ancients, however, we cannot undo the problem by a single bold stroke. Rather, by analogy, the knot must be *untied* painstakingly. Many interrelated steps are involved in this process, but the first and foremost of these is to change the yardstick of classroom success. Simply put, success must be viewed—as Ferdinand Hoppe did so long ago—in terms of exceeding one's *own* standards rather than surpassing the performance of others. The experimental analogue of this process is Hoppe's research on level of aspiration (see Chapter 2). There success (and failure) was an individual matter, largely independent of the achievements of others, with the frequency of success depending on the setting of realistic self-goals.

Basically, we are arguing that students should take charge of certain important aspects of their own learning. This involves not so much choosing *what* they will learn—for there is still a broad consensus as to what skills are necessary for survival in our society—but rather it involves freedom of choice in *how* to learn. This means allowing students more responsibility in setting their own performance standards, levels of aspiration, and the pace at which they will learn. To allow this kind of freedom, learning must be structured so that it becomes a process of goal setting toward individual, academic objectives. In effect, the student takes responsibility for his own progress with his aspirations always in advance of current achievement, yet not so far ahead that they cannot be attained through persistent effort and practice.

Once Hoppe's self-protective mechanism (see p. 20) is free to operate, students can control their own rate of learning, and—most importantly—the incidence of success and failure. With a more adequate supply of self-rewards assured, the student can hope to become more success-oriented—that is, disposed to work for successes rather than compelled to avoid disapproval. Moreover, sufficient rewards mean a reduction in defensive maneuvering to the extent that each student is able to succeed on his own. But, of course, these successes must be valued by the individual. Meaningless successes cannot long sustain a sense of positive self-regard. Might not the fact that successes are no longer scarce cheapen their meaning? Hopefully not. Scarcity is largely a phenomenon of peer-group competition. Once the focus shifts toward individual striving, the value of a success depends less on its frequency and more on the risk the individual runs to achieve it. The only way to devalue success in this context is to set one's goals so low that success is virtually assured. Happily, the available research suggests this does not happen. When individuals are not competing directly with one another, they usually tend to set moderate learning goals slightly beyond their current performance level (Lewin *et al.*, 1944, p. 337). Thus, students in the same classroom can derive satisfaction from struggling against challenging odds, simultaneously and despite the fact that each is achieving at a different level.

Note, too, that positive rewards still come from successful performance. Achievement is still of paramount value. It is only the *measure* of achievement that has changed, not its importance. And with this transformation the scale of classroom values tips in favor of such personal qualities as effort, good judgment, and industry, and away from a preoccupation with ability as the ultimate measure of one's worth. In sum, teachers must promote two kinds of excellence. As John Gardner (1961) puts it,

There is a way of measuring excellence that involves comparison between people—some are musical geniuses and some are not; and there is another that involves comparison between myself at my best and myself at my worst. It is this latter comparison which enables me to assert that I am being true to the best that is in me—or forces me to confess that I am not [p. 128].

An appreciation for such individual excellence is nothing new. Society has always recognized that it benefits not only from those who have achieved excellence but also from those who are trying. And, despite some appearances to the contrary, schools believe this also. Teachers report that they reward effort more than ability; and to the extent that this is actually carried out in practice, it is a noble sentiment. But we also appreciate just how long the odds are against this strategy working. First of all, teachers are only human; they sometimes do not, or cannot, practice what they believe. Witness the research on self-fulfilling prophecy that documents how teachers often unwittingly favor their more successful students, despite philosophical values to the contrary. Moreover, when teachers do manage to encourage students to strive for accomplishments within their grasp, students are not always receptive. Teacher praise is discounted by many students because they believe themselves incapable of praiseworthy actions; success is rejected because of the implied obligation to do even better the next time; and if this were not enough, the teacher's motivation in praising students may become suspect.

All in all, fostering individual excellence is an exceedingly difficult proposition. Accepting one's limitations is a good case in point. We have made much of the pattern of negative attributions found in low-esteem students, especially the tendency to blame failure on low ability. Fortunately, there is some evidence that such students can be trained to increase their problem-solving efforts before assuming the worst about themselves (see Dweck, 1975). This is a most encouraging development, but there is another side to the issue. Failure does *not* always imply insufficient effort. Sometimes it signals that personal limits have been reached and that all the confidence and persistence in the world will not change things.

This leads us to a vital conclusion. Accepting one's limits gracefully is as important as learning to overcome them. There is a truism that states that no one is perfect, and certainly no one is perfect at everything he undertakes. Yet, despite the obviousness of this remark, many students are threatened by less than perfect performances, especially if perfection is necessary to feel worthy. Students must be helped to accept their limitations without devaluing themselves or destroying their will to learn. But more than mere acceptance, students must be encouraged to actually *seek out* and test their limits. Only in this way can they maintain realistic aspirations in the long run. However, this can be achieved only by changing the conditions of learning so that students are deliberately rewarded for recognizing and working at tasks within their reach but beyond their current achievement. If competitive learning has made accepting one's limits loathsome, even intolerable, then hopefully the process can be reversed or at least curbed by altering the conditions of classroom learning.

Consider a simple example of how such alterations might work. For all the good-natured fun and excitement it generates, the "spelling bee" is in many ways the epitome of classroom competition. By necessity there is *the* winner (usually a girl). There are also several near-winners, and the rest are losers to one degree or another. Yet by introducing only modest changes, one researcher has transformed this game into an object lesson in the importance of recognizing and working within one's limits (de Charms, 1972). Rather than assigning spelling words to students on a random basis as is usually the case, this experimenter gave each student a choice of three kinds of words to spell: easy, moderately difficult, and difficult. Students were kept from automatically choosing an easy word because spelling it gave their team only one point, whereas spelling the moderately difficult word meant two points, and three points were given for the hard words. Naturally, the incorrect spelling of any word resulted in no points. The scale of difficulty was tailored to each individual. Easy words were those that the student had spelled correctly on a test several days before; moderately difficult words were those he had misspelled but had studied in the meantime; and hard words were taken from the next spelling assignment, which no student had yet seen. By this arrangement students quickly learned that success depends on a careful evaluation of one's own skills—in this case, spelling skills—and that if they disregard these realities, no matter how bright they might be, they penalize themselves by failing. Moreover, they learned that a realistic goal is the most challenging kind and incidentally the one that yields the greatest payoff.

These lessons must be learned if students are ever to become self-accepting. But rarely are they taught for in school, nor *can* they be unless the structure of learning is changed. The good will of the teacher is simply not enough. These lessons must be institutionalized in the learning process itself. It must be repeatedly demonstrated that there are payoffs for realistic self-appraisal and penalties for unrealistic self-appraisal. Moreover, these efforts must not be viewed as merely a patronizing gesture—a kind of sop—to the less able in the hope that inequality will somehow be more bearable. Ability aside, learning to accept limits is a vital goal in its own right, for everyone. Indeed, contemporary clinical psychology recognizes self-acceptance as an indispensable ingredient to healthy life adjustment. Research on the discrepancy between ideal-self and actual-self (see Chapter 3) bears this out.

From all that has gone before, we can conclude that fostering a sense of self-worth and achievement in the schools involves a two-fold process. First, teachers must encourage students to maintain a match between their aspirations and current abilities so that individual successes will become more likely. And second, teachers must promote a willingness among students to accept these increased successes, for the pursuit of personal excellence depends as much on a capacity for positive self-reinforcement as it does on the occurrence of rewards in the first place.

For the remainder of this chapter we will explore how individual goal setting promotes these twin objectives. In the following chapter we will consider the kinds of achievement skills necessary to sustain success once an achievement-orientation is established and ways that these skills can be taught for in the classroom.

Achievement-oriented Structures

Within the past decade educational psychology has witnessed the beginning of a vigorous, almost explosive effort to study the benefits of individual goal setting in learning. Indeed, this enterprise is still gaining momentum. Although the research is as yet scattered and largely at an exploratory stage, the available evidence is encouraging. It suggests that learning can be arranged in ways that reduce the threat to self-worth and, consequently, increase individual and group achievement. Examples of some of the most promising current research efforts are described in the following sections.

Individual Success Striving. Alfred Alschuler and his colleagues have attempted to solve the problem of insufficient classroom rewards by rewarding realistic academic goal setting among students. To use Alschuler's own terminology once again, this is accomplished by modifying "the rules of the learning game." The ingenuity and success of this approach is well illustrated by the transformation of one fifth grade mathematics class (Alschuler, 1969). In this particular class the learning climate had been competitive, yet boring. In an unwavering daily routine the teacher would first discuss the homework from the previous day, then lecture on the new material, which in turn became the basis for the next homework assignment. Needless to say, many students demonstrated a superb capacity for passive resistance and maneuvering of the kind we have come to recognize as failure-avoiding. The alterations in this learning structure were relatively simple ones but were profound in their impact. Students still continued to work through the assigned textbook on a chapter-by-chapter basis, but with a difference. Each student was now encouraged to work at his own individual pace, spending as much or as little time as needed to master the material. Proficiency tests were administered at the end of each chapter. To ensure that each student worked up to his individual capacity, a system of rewards was introduced by which the youngsters were paid for the number of test problems they got right. The coin of the realm was monopoly money. In addition, a goal-setting element was introduced by requiring students to indicate what percentage of test problems they would work to get correct. A realistic estimate was vital since a student would lose money if he either overestimated or underestimated his performance on the test. Thus success came to depend as much on an accurate match between aspirations and current understanding as it did on performance alone. Moreover, since the object was to maximize earnings, students consistently set their goals at or near the upper reach of ability.

From what can be recalled of the research on level of

aspiration and the dynamics of goal setting, we would predict a progressive increase in achievement in this situation. And this is precisely what happened. The *degree* of improvement was the only surprise and a pleasant one at that. The average mathematics achievement score for these youngsters increased nearly three grade levels during the school year! They had begun to assess themselves more optimistically and performed up to these self-imposed expectations. In short, they had become success-oriented. Interestingly, these were the same students who the year before had made only minuscule gains in mathematics achievement under the same teacher. Restructuring made the difference!

This experiment also neatly illustrates the interaction between intrinsic and extrinsic motivation. The extrinsic fascination of playing a game sustained student interest long enough for these youngsters to master sufficient skills so that the act of solving math problems became satisfying in its own right. At that point the play money began to lose much of its former value, and grasping entrepreneurs gave way to dedicated mathematics students. We can gauge something of the strength of this intrinsic involvement by the fact that students who had done nothing the previous year, except under threat, suddenly began taking their books home on the weekends, few students missed assignments, and all expressed an increased liking for mathematics.

The process of fostering a will to learn depends, in the short run, on mastery of the underlying academic skills. But once a basic facility is established, a natural shift occurs and performance comes more and more under intrinsic control. This metamorphosis is vividly demonstrated by the work of Harold Cohen and James Filipczak (1971) with juvenile delinquents. These boys were given tokens as rewards for successful completion of work assignments in reading and mathematics. The tokens could then be exchanged for various privileges such as ordering things from the Sears and Roebuck catalogue. At first the mail-order business was brisk. But as scores on standardized achievement tests began to rise, the boys showed a marked change in how they spent their tokens. No longer solely content with material rewards, the boys began to purchase library time and pay rent on individual study cubicles. Learning itself had become a sought-after goal.

The Center School. The Center School of New Canaan, Connecticut, embodies many of the principles under investigation by Alfred Alschuler with the same positive results, but this time on a much larger scale involving an entire elementary school. This public school experiment began about ten years ago under the direction of Stephen Rubin. Each student in the school learns in a highly individualized manner within an achievement-oriented structure.

To create this structure Rubin and his staff first selected the subjects that most schools teach and then analyzed the learning process involved in each of them. This meant identifying a progression of learning steps or skills—something akin to building blocks—that the student must master in order to perform at the next higher level of proficiency. For example, in the field of mathematics Rubin identified hundreds of objectives ranging from recognizing numbers to solving quadratic equations. Once the learning path was established for each subject, the school staff constructed a step-by-step curriculum designed to help students master the content at top efficiency.

Individual students are given an opportunity to make their own way within the structure of learning steps for each subject. As in traditional schools, the students work simultaneously in all subject-matter fields, but at Center School this work is done at different rates and at different levels of placement depending on abilities and the willingness to study. Typically students work on one objective at a time within small groups of students who, irrespective of age or grade, are at the same level of mastery for a particular subject. Students progress from one step to another by passing a proficiency test that they themselves schedule whenever they feel ready. In this way individual goal setting is made an integral part of the learning process.

As another consequence of this system, a youngster's classmates are continually changing. One unexpected benefit of this is that these small groups retain a task-oriented character—their purpose being the serious business of learning—rather than becoming a primary social grouping as happens in most classrooms where learning is subordinated to the pursuit of friendships, establishing social roles, and, more ominously, where competitive expectations emerge along with an intellectual pecking order. Yet the important values of sociability and mutual cooperation are not neglected. Each student spends about 40 percent of his time in a permanent homeroom with students his own age. Thus Center School combines the philosophies of both graded and nongraded classrooms.

Academically, the results are impressive. Students of average IQ perform consistently above the national average on standardized achievement tests, and this superiority increases steadily until by the sixth grade a near-majority are achieving at a level expected of ninth grade students. But, as we know, the mere fact of high achievement is not as significant as the motives behind it. Although there is no direct evidence that students are motivated by a success-orientation, certain facts do strongly suggest that this *is* the case: the virtual absence of disciplinary problems in the school, an exceedingly low rate of absenteeism, and a continued enthusiasm for learning among students of all ability levels (Rubin, 1975).

Contingency Contracting. The essence of Center School has been captured and miniaturized in a form that can be used by individual teachers without the elaborate restructuring of an entire school. Called *contingency contracting*, this technique involves establishing work contracts between a teacher and individual students (Homme, 1970). Work contracts can vary in scope, complexity, and duration depending on their purpose. There is, for instance, the brief *micro*-contract, which may involve learning only one small step in the long march toward a significant achievement, such as the mastery of long division. There is also the long-range contract whose fulfillment depends on learning long division itself, that is to say, mastering and integrating *all* of the many intervening skill steps. Lloyd Homme calls this a *macro*-contract. Establishing work contracts, both large and small, involves a clear statement of what the student is to do, negotiating the amount and/or quality of work required, as well as indicating what the payoff will be when the student meets these conditions. Sometimes the payoff is a grade. Other times it can simply be the opportunity to do additional schoolwork, but of a kind the student finds intrinsically more interesting than the original assignment (e.g., "first complete these ten arithmetic problems, then you may read the next chapter in *Huckleberry Finn*"). Other powerful motivating techniques include allowing students free time to spend as they wish once their assignment is finished (Osborne, 1969). The term *contingency contracting* derives from the fact that rewards of educational value are *contingent* on the successful completion of a contract.

Contingency contracting as a technique has a number of important characteristics. It is essentially noncompetitive, and, if monitored with reasonable care, it permits a matching between task difficulty and current skill level. This means that success will not only be more frequent but will come to depend largely on the amount and quality of effort expended. Moreover, it promotes greater clarity regarding what is expected of the student and spells out the learning steps needed to reach the goal. This reinforces a task orientation where the emphasis is on *accomplishment* rather than on avoiding the teacher's disapproval. Furthermore, the rewards can be individualized to reflect each student's progression from extrinsic to intrinsic motivation. Indeed, as envisioned by Homme, the long-range objective is to lead the student to initiate his own personal contracts and then to reward himself for completing them, in effect, to become a self-sustaining, autonomous achiever. The evidence suggests that with proper guidance students can learn to do this.

Of special interest here is the finding that when students establish and administer their own schedule of self-reinforcement, their learning increases at a faster rate than when success is rewarded by the teacher (Lovitt and Curtiss, 1969). This finding makes good sense in light of research reviewed earlier in Chapter 2. You will recall that teacher praise does little to motivate if it is dispensed for performances that fall below the student's own standards. Naturally, it is the student who can best evaluate the quality of his striving on a moment-to-moment basis. He knows how often and to what extent he is deserving and can praise himself on those fleeting occasions that would otherwise escape the teacher's notice.

The innovative curriculum experiments reported in this section share individual goal setting as a common element. There is also another important similarity. Each provides for well-stated objectives and clarity of learning steps, a topic to which we now turn.

Clarity, Absolute Standards, and Achievement

Students need to know where they are going, how best to get there, and how far they have yet to go. Clarity of educational goals and of the learning steps needed to attain them stimulates achievement striving. Yet all too frequently students go uninformed as to exactly what material they must learn. They also seldom see examples of the kinds of skill levels they are expected to attain and upon which their evaluation will be based. The fact that the student is graded periodically is only of marginal help in providing proper guidance since grades are notoriously poor indicators of the quality of a student's work. This is because grades tend to be too global to be diagnostic. Moreover, they are often used for purposes other than conveying information. One common practice is to use grades in an effort to motivate students. But if a student is given a *C* instead of an *F* to "encourage him," he will be misled on the vital question of how he is actually doing. Likewise, if the grade reflects the teacher's total impression of the student and takes into account such extraneous factors as his willingness to comply with authority, his degree of classroom participation, and his personal neatness, then the student will also be misled.

The kinds of precision needed for setting proper standards and for effective guidance are illustrated by the concept of *absolute performance standards*. Here the teacher identifies what it is students should learn, establishes the level of proficiency they must reach, and—most important —teaches toward these objectives. Often the objectives are couched in terms of the specific learning behaviors expected, a practice commonly referred to as "established behavioral objectives."

As an example of this process, consider a ninth grade American literature class. These students read several short stories each week and then prepare book reports. At the beginning of the school year the teacher conveyed his idea of a good report by providing the students with sample reports ranging in quality from excellent to acceptable to unacceptable. By comparing these samples, students discovered the set of criteria by which their work would be judged. These criteria covered such factors as length of the report and the depth of analysis required. Reports that fell below the minimally acceptable standards were returned to students to be redone; reports meeting or surpassing the standards were given full credit. As a sophisticated twist on the notion of absolute standards, the teacher periodically produced additional samples that represented somewhat higher minimal standards. Naturally the teacher taught toward these more demanding objectives, for example, by teaching students to recognize various literary devices commonly used by writers and discussing the concepts of plot and character development.

Not only do absolute standards clarify objectives, but,

like individual goal setting, they make learning more task-oriented. Success depends on mastering the task at hand rather than on doing better than someone else. In fact, any number of students can succeed as long as they all meet the standards. Moreover, absolute standards tend to foster a positive interpretation of failure. After reviewing a large body of research, Kennedy and Willcutt (1964, p. 329) concluded that when a well-defined standard of performance is expected of students, failure to achieve that standard tends to motivate them to try harder. In contrast, when the teacher's evaluative comments focus only on the performance itself without any references to external standards, then failure tends to lower motivation. In the first instance, failure implies falling short of a goal, while in the second it seems to imply falling short as a person!

Combining absolute standards with individual student goal setting creates a powerful structure for fostering achievement motivation. Under this arrangement a student sets a series of intermediate subgoals as he works toward the more distant final objective, with the result that success at each step sustains the student in his drive for top proficiency. This is similar to Homme's notion of a macro-contract.

An example of this process is provided once again by Alfred Alschuler and his colleagues (1969). This time these researchers restructured a high school typing class. The final course grade was determined by the number of words per minute typed correctly at the end of the school year, so many words for an *A*, so many for a *B*, and so on. The student's task was to strive against these absolute performance standards through a combination of typing practice and almost daily goal setting. After a practice session each student was encouraged to set a new scoring goal for himself in light of his current typing rate. This goal could be stated in terms of words per minute and/or the difficulty level of the passage to be typed. Each student then decided when to take the next typing test, depending on how much practice he estimated would be needed to achieve his latest goal. You will probably recognize that this arrangement is almost an exact analogue to Ferdinand Hoppe's laboratory research on level of aspiration. Here, as in Hoppe's experiments, the likelihood of success—that is, the chances of exceeding one's aspirations—depended on setting realistic goals in view of current performance, the difficulty of the passage to be typed, and the amount of practice deemed necessary.

In a comparison class taught by the same instructor, other students were allowed none of this personal decision making. Typing tests were of uniform difficulty level and were administered to all students at a time chosen by the teacher. The average typing proficiency of these comparison students showed little improvement over the school year, while the performance of the experimental students increased steadily until by the end of the year this group was typing an average of 54 percent more words per minute than they had been at the beginning. It was the frequency of their personal successes—and occasional failures—that sustained an upward spiral of typing proficiency in these students.

A number of other studies confirm that clearly stated objectives lead to increased achievement and that it is the anxious, failure-prone student who benefits most from such clarity. In the absence of sufficient structure these students perform poorly, and things worsen when ambiguity occurs in an atmosphere of personal evaluation. What seems most critical for these pupils is knowledge of how well they are doing, often termed "knowledge of results" by psychologists. Without such information or feedback, fearful students suspect the worst and tend to prejudge their performance as unacceptable (Meunier and Rule, 1967). They fall victim to their own sense of inadequacy and, as a consequence, become overdependent on the judgments of others regarding the value of their work. However, if learning is properly structured, anxious students can perform as well as and sometimes even better than less anxious ones (Campeau, 1968; Noll, 1955). These results are achieved in several ways: by arranging the material to be learned in a series of steps, from easy to difficult; by making explicit the connections between one task and the next and then explaining how they all fit together into a larger whole; and, of course, by providing immediate and continual feedback regarding the student's progress.

One of the most ambitious efforts to structure learning in these ways is reported by Grimes and Allinsmith (1961). These researchers modified a conventional reading program for the first three primary grades in an effort to achieve greater clarity of work demands. At the end of three years it was found that students using the restructured version were reading above grade level with high-anxiety students in the group performing best of all! In marked contrast a matched group of comparison students using the conventional "unstructured" program were reading well below grade level with anxious students performing the poorest. From this we may conclude that failure-prone students are influenced far more than are other students—both for good and ill—by the conditions of learning and that one key to their success is clarity of means and ends. For a further discussion of the importance of clearly stated learning objectives, see the Gagné (1974) volume in this series.

Self-confidence, Ability Level, and Achievement

When individuals are free to do so, they set their aspirations at or near the upper reaches of their ability. As Hoppe and others have discovered, this produces an upward spiraling of both self-expectations and performance with the result that achievement is maximized for students at *every* ability level. This dynamic helps to explain the dramatic increases we have noted in achievement scores when students work under conditions of individual goal setting.

The uplifting effect on achievement caused by matching ability and expectations is convincingly demonstrated in a recent study by Charles Woodson (1975). Several hundred junior high students were divided into five ability levels. Just prior to receiving training in various subject-matter topics, the students were administered a test to illustrate the kinds of things they would be required to learn. Unknown to them, there were three forms of the test: one form was difficult, another moderately difficult, and the third was easy. By administering these sample tests, the experimenter, in effect, set the performance standards by which the students expected to be judged. Within each of the ability levels, one-third of the students received the easy test; another third, the moderately difficult test; and the last third, the difficult test. In this way, 15 groups were created with varying degrees of mismatch between their ability level and the severity of standards required. At the end of the training period, all students were given another test designed to show how much material they had learned. The findings indicated that the amount learned depended on how close the match was between ability and performance standards. Students who enjoyed a close or perfect match learned the most, and this was true at all ability levels. In contrast, a mismatch disrupted learning at all ability levels. This occurred because the less able students who were saddled with high expectations became demoralized and simply gave up, while highly able pupils who competed against easy standards became bored. As a consequence, both these groups became underachievers, though for different reasons. Similar research at the college level also indicates that maximum effort is exerted by students when they are given tests within the average range of difficulty, neither too easy nor too hard (Marso, 1969). Also, for these same students there was evidence of increased retention of the material tested.

Not only does striving against challenging standards enhance performance, but the evidence indicates that it also promotes a sense of personal satisfaction and positive self-regard. Martin Covington and his colleagues are presently investigating those teaching conditions that yield an optimal combination of high performance and a sense of pride in accomplishment (Covington and Jacoby, 1973; Covington and Polsky, 1974; and Schnur, 1975).

In one study several hundred college students took part in an introductory psychology course that required them to complete various work projects. These projects required each student to create his own solutions to a number of substantive issues, problems, and dilemmas confronting contemporary psychology (Covington and Jacoby, 1972). While all students worked on the same projects, different levels of excellence were expected. One group of students was given full credit for their projects as long as the work met a minimum standard of quality. Since this level was well within the capacity of virtually all students, a high course grade could be obtained by effort alone ("effort only" group). A second group was required to strive against standards of excellence commensurate with the grade they desired—that is, the standards were quite stringent for an *A*, somewhat less demanding for a *B*, and so on. Since performance at the higher levels required a greater exercise of ability and skill in the form of ingenuity, logical analysis, and imagination, we can say that success for these students depended on a combination of effort *and* ability ("effort × ability" group). Virtually all students in both groups set as their personal goal a final course grade of *A*.

The resulting quality of work among the "effort only" group was low. This is hardly surprising in light of what we know about the relationship between level of performance and work standards. The lower standards simply bred mediocre performance, and, as a consequence, these students were generally disappointed with the quality of their work and felt undeserving of their high grade. In contrast, the performance of the "effort × ability" group was markedly higher, obviously due to the higher standards demanded. But what was not as predictable was the attitudes of these students about their performance. Even though the "effort × ability" group worked harder and longer to get the same grades as the first group, they were nonetheless more satisfied with their performances, believed they measured up favorably to the instructor's expectations, and felt more deserving of their grades.

Thus working hard to achieve one's goals at some risk of failure not only seems to increase the quality of performance but also the degree of satisfaction once the goal is attained. In short, goals that are challenging and require hard work are seen as more valuable. The "easy *A*" does little to enhance a sense of competency. From these data it appears that it is not the grade per se that affects the student's sense of accomplishment, but rather what he has to do to get the grade. The important conclusion to be drawn from these several studies is that realistic goal setting is a prime ingredient in fostering the growth of both confidence and competency, simultaneously and at all ability levels.

Attributions, Task Analysis, and Effort

Realistic goal setting also strengthens the proper attributions regarding the causes of success and failure. When an individual works on a task within his reach, degree of effort becomes the overriding determinant of success (and failure). Thus, if the student falls short of his goal, then blame more naturally goes to insufficient effort since the task *was* manageable. By the same token, success is seen as being the outcome of skillful effort. In short, the student learns that "I can do it if I try." This is precisely the same conclusion the teacher attempts to engineer through rewarding effort. Here, then, students and teacher converge toward the same means and end—individual achievement through personal effort.

Yet the failure-prone student is likely to remain unconvinced since he largely discounts personal effort as a cause of success for, try as he might, he often ends up failing. Of course, this is because his efforts are misplaced and wasteful. What this student needs in addition to practice in proper goal setting is training in effective thinking so that his efforts will begin to count for something.

One important aspect of this training is *task analysis*. The student will find it helpful to analyze his work assignments to determine what makes them difficult and then take steps to overcome these obstacles. The previous example of restructuring a high school typing class (see p. 104) illustrates the use and value of such task analysis. Students inspected all of the typing material well in advance of the periodic tests. Difficult stroke and letter combinations were identified and solutions discussed by the group.

Learning how to make a difficult task easier has several advantages. For one, it increases the student's sense of being the agent of his own successes. It also discourages improper effort and focuses attention on the true obstacles in learning—the current limitations of the individual and the complexity of the task. Moreover, altering task difficulty permits the student to improve the odds for success without necessarily lowering aspirations. Furthermore, there is less reason for the student to avoid genuine effort for fear that it will reflect on his ability should he fail. Other interpretations of failure are now possible. A combination of high effort and failure may occur because initial aspirations were set unrealistically high, or the task was improperly analyzed, or perhaps the student simply gave up too soon. These are constructive interpretations of failure in that they point to factors within the student's power to correct. They are also task-oriented and consequently do not lead to the kinds of self-doubt and paralysis caused by defensive excuses designed to protect a sense of worth. In effect, the student has gained the "freedom to fail" even after having tried hard. And with this freedom there is less need to employ self-deceptive tactics.

In sum, then, moderate goal setting and task analysis reinforce the causal link between personal effort and outcome and help combat a sense of learned helplessness. But what of the tendency among some students to deny their successes by attributing them to a lucky break or to the humanitarian impulses of a teacher? Or what of those students who on occasion even sabotage their own efforts? How can these dispositions be combated?

Given their importance, it is surprising how little attention these questions have received in the research literature. To date only David Mettee (1971) has offered any advice in the matter. Mettee speculates that eventually individuals might be persuaded to assume responsibility for their successes if they first begin by accepting only partial credit—just enough to raise their confidence without arousing threat. Presumably, as the person becomes more comfortable with success and realizes how satisfying it can be, he will take more and more of the credit. Unfortunately, no practical demonstration of this idea has yet been made. Another somewhat different solution is suggested by the nature of the threat. We have argued that some individuals desperately want to accept credit but dare not because of the consequences. The threat is that others will come to expect further success, something the individual doubts his ability to do. Faced with this cruel conflict between desiring and fearing success, the individual simply gives up claim to his achievement. The implication is that success threatens because it cannot be reproduced. But if the student can bring his achievements under control through a combination of realistic goal setting, task analysis, and proper effort, then success *is* repeatable. Under the circumstances we can hope that the student will not only accept credit for his accomplishment but will also express optimism about the chances for future success as well.

Teacher-Student Relations

We have portrayed teachers and students as opponents in the competitive learning game—teachers have the authority to dispense and withhold rewards and students the capacity to resist and sabotage learning. If it is true, as we have argued, that the cause of student demoralization resides in the relationship between teachers and students, then altering the learning rules so that power is shared ought to bring about swift, even dramatic, changes for the better. Indeed, the research we have reviewed thus far confirms this. Yet many teachers are threatened by the idea of sharing power, especially if they already feel impotent in the face of grudging, disobedient students. What these teachers need—they will tell you—is more, not less, power. Here it becomes necessary to sensitize teachers to the ways in which they and their students antagonize one another. Hopefully such insights will lead to collaborative efforts to restructure learning in more humanizing ways.

One of the most ambitious attempts to do this involved training the entire staff of an urban junior high school in what Alfred Alschuler has called "social relations literacy" (1975). Over a two-year period, Alschuler and his colleagues encouraged teachers and students to analyze the dynamics of the *discipline game* (see p. 30) and to identify the moves, countermoves, and cycles that disrupt learning. As teachers began to realize that their authority to control student attention and effort is severely limited under most circumstances—their only power being the power to punish—resistance slowly gave way to a spirit of experimentation. One classroom after another set about creating new social relation rules by which mutual goals could be achieved. For the teacher this meant more opportunity to teach and for the student, more freedom to learn on his own. A number of different learning structures evolved, each uniquely suited to the requirements of the particular subject matter taught. Yet, despite all the diversity, there emerged a common theme. Most restructuring involved setting time aside—best described as "mutually agreed learning time"—during which teacher and students had one another's undivided attention.

In a similar spirit, Arthur Pearl (see Silberman, 1970, p. 346) altered conditions of learning so that he and his students—high school dropouts and migrant workers—

shared joint responsibility for learning. A contract system was established at the beginning of the course in which Pearl and each student negotiated dates on which examinations would be taken for each unit of work. Contracts could be renegotiated if the student felt he was not ready at the agreed upon time, as long as there was good reason. In the event that a student failed to meet the minimal test standards, he had the option of taking the test again after further study. Moreover, any grade could be appealed if the student felt that it did not fairly reflect his knowledge and understanding of the topic. Pearl contends that once there is some procedure for handling such grievances, teachers and students can become partners instead of adversaries.

Cooperative arrangements such as those encouraged by Pearl and Alschuler make for many subtle but important changes in the ways teachers relate to students. Nowhere is this better illustrated than in the distinction between praise and encouragement (see Coopersmith and Feldman, 1974). Praise is the dominant response of the power-oriented classroom. Praise is a global endorsement of the person, a vote of support, so to speak—"You are good because you did what I asked." This kind of message has several undesirable consequences. For one thing, we know that praise can act as an external reward and can corrupt intrinsic motivation, turning play into work. This is especially likely when praise is used in nonspecific ways, and to excess as a motivating device. For another thing, praise focuses on the person and not on his accomplishments, thereby increasing student dependency on the teacher as his main source of self-confidence. Earlier in this chapter we noted that such an overreliance on the judgment of others can be disastrous for the failure-avoiding student.

In contrast, *encouragement* focuses on the student's own standards, his pace and progress toward mastery, and on the ways he can improve. To paraphrase Stanley Coopersmith and Ronald Feldman (1974), encouragement says, in effect, "Here are some ways to do even better next time."

Such messages tend to encourage confidence and accelerate achievement. This is illustrated in a classic study by Ellis Page (1958). Page asked a number of junior high teachers to return test papers to the students containing one of three kinds of feedback: (1) the grade only; (2) the grade accompanied by a brief supportive comment (e.g., "Good work. Keep it up."); or (3) comments that were not only accepting of the student but also identified specific strengths and weaknesses in his performance. Page found that the students who were given encouragement through specific positive and negative information (the third group) showed the greatest improvement on subsequent tests.

Encouragement as a teaching style is most compatible with the achievement-oriented classroom where the emphasis is on realistic student goal setting, task analysis, and, above all, on learning as a cooperative venture.

Grading Policy and Practices

Some observers (see Kindsvatter, 1969) believe that the only major improvement in grading method in this century occurred during the years 1913–18. At that time Daniel Starch conducted several studies that demonstrated the tremendous variation—more aptly described as chaos—in the kinds of rationale teachers used to grade students. For example, in the public schools of Illinois alone, over 100 different grading systems were in use. Starch proposed to correct this situation by employing the now familiar normal curve, which provided a statistical basis for grading and incidentally introduced the *ABCDF* system of grading symbols. Since 1918 there has been no basic change in grading practices in the United States and, until recently, little serious questioning of the psychological consequences of "grading on the curve." Of course, all that has now changed. Indifference has been replaced by concern and, in some quarters, by anger. Critics are numerous, articulate, and, on the whole, correct. Their agitation is forcing a reexamination of traditional grading practices with the result that new forms are emerging, many of which hold considerable promise for fostering individual excellence.

The main objection to "grading on the curve" is that it automatically makes some students successful at the expense of others and breeds a condition of scarcity of rewards. Like success and failure, grades also follow the laws of commodity theory—the less frequent a good grade, the more sought after and valuable it becomes. Indeed, grades are really nothing more than success and failure made official and public. It is for this reason that grades become so threatening. Parents and teachers stress the importance of grades so much that students come to feel as good or as bad as their grades appear.

Because grades are so valued for their own sake, they become obstacles to learning. Most students do whatever is necessary to obtain the highest grades possible. The result is that the teacher's grading methods control almost everything about a student's work: what he does in class, how he does it, and what he pays attention to. Unfortunately, students quite often concentrate on the wrong things. Many of them spend nearly as much time trying to beat the grading system as they devote to actual studying. This preoccupation with grades tends to force a slavish conformity on students and reinforces informal sanctions against speculation, innovative thinking, and intellectual risk taking. Students tend to perform for the short-run advantages of external rewards, which divert their attention from the real values of learning. Grading also handicaps the teacher. It forces him to teach things that are more easily measured and tested. Moreover, it tends to cast the teacher in the role of a punishing authority rather than as a facilitator of learning.

Grades as motivators. Grading is frequently defended on the grounds that it serves to motivate learning. But, as we have noted, grades are most apt to motivate students for the wrong reasons and, in the end, pervert the true purpose of learning. Moreover, the research evidence on the value of grades as motivators is not encouraging. Lewis Goldberg (1965) scored college midterm examinations according to several different grading policies. The purpose was to determine which, if any, of these strategies would motivate students to exert the greater effort on a later examination. For one group of students, Goldberg graded leniently, on the assumption that positive reinforcement motivates achievement best. For another group, he graded strictly, on the theory that punishment in the form of low grades is the best motivational inducement. For a third group, he created a *discrepancy* between the expected grade and the one the student received by giving a disproportionately large number of *A*s and *F*s. According to this model, it is the discrepancy and not reward or punishment per se that motivates achievement. Presumably, those students who unexpectedly get an *A* will work hard to keep it, while students whose performances are unexpectedly poor will work hard to improve. As it turned out, there were no differences in the subsequent test performances of any of these groups; nor did their performances differ from those of groups graded on the traditional "normal" curve. Thus, it appears that grading policies differ little in their motivational impact on student achievement. This is not to say that a specific grade cannot be used as a "reward" or "punishment" for a particular student. But the results of doing this are often unpredictable and frustrating. Kirschenbaum and his colleagues (1971) pinpoint the reason for this. Grades tend to motivate those students who *least* need it, that is, those who are already successful; while, perversely, the very students who need motivating the most (poor students) are most put off and threatened by grades (Child and Whiting, 1949; Shaw and McCuen, 1960). The explanation for this is clear enough when we recall that successful students are motivated by both positive *and* negative feedback, while for the poor student an unexpected success is often met with disbelief, if not suspicion, and a bad grade simply confirms his low self-image.

Actually, of course, grades do accomplish certain things. The threat of a poor grade forces students to pay attention and causes them to undertake work they otherwise might not do. But the use of grades for such negative reasons further reinforces failure avoidance. In effect, the student must behave in a satisfactory manner to escape the teacher's disapproval. Yet we can also sympathize with the teacher. All too often the exasperated teacher finds that grades are the only means available for controlling classroom behavior and for maintaining some semblance of order, and, of course, without order no learning is possible. It is at such times that teachers refer apologetically to grading as a "necessary evil." Thus it is that the threat of a poor grade—like the threat of being sent to the principal's office—becomes a weapon to overcome student resistance, apathy, and mediocre effort. But, as we have seen, all of these may be signs of student defensiveness, and to use grades to deal with these symptoms simply compounds the problem.

When it comes to motivating school achievement, it appears that the type of learning structure is by far the more important factor, with grades playing a secondary, even negligible, role. For example, it has been shown that under *competitive* conditions student achievement is depressed whether grades are given or not (Alschuler, 1969). In this case, the presence of grades simply aggravates the situation by placing still further limits on an already dwindling supply of rewards, while the absence of grades deprives the teacher of any control whatsoever. On the other hand, there is evidence that achievement can be sustained for long periods of time in the absence of formal grading as long as an achievement motive has been aroused in the student (Alschuler, 1969; Chamberlain *et al.*, 1942). Moreover, once a success orientation is established, the reintroduction of grades may actually aid learning. This is because the purpose of grading is transformed from that of providing a (dubious) source of motivation and control to that of providing information to the learner.

Grades as information. With achievement structures energizing the will to learn, the teacher can be freer to use grading in a more innovative and flexible fashion to accomplish its true purpose, that of providing feedback to the student regarding the quality of his work and ways he can further improve. In the long run this will allow the student to gain an accurate picture of his individual pattern of strengths and weaknesses.

Grading is most likely to make a positive contribution if it is to some degree under the control of the person being evaluated and if there is some guarantee against total failure for taking intellectual risks. One obvious way to insure against complete failure is for the teacher to set a floor under the grades so that a minimum grade, say, an average *C* is assured for meeting the basic requirements (Harrison, 1969). In terms of absolute standards this might mean establishing the minimal level of mastery acceptable to the teacher. As to the matter of permitting some student control over grades, there are a number of possibilities. A student might decide beforehand the kinds of performances on which he wished to be judged, for example, by choosing to undertake some work options but not others. Or he might be evaluated in part on the extent to which he fulfilled specific work goals he set for himself at the beginning of his study. Or he could be more directly involved in actual grading decisions, either through self-grading or by a process of joint grading between the teacher and the student in which the final grade is an average of the two. It is noteworthy that when the student has available the teacher's criteria for good performance and grades himself according to them, self-assigned grades in most cases do not differ substantially from the teacher's grade (Anderson, 1966). This suggests that under proper guidance, students can practice the skills of self-evaluation without abusing the privilege.

Placed in this context of self-appraisal and personal decision making, the issue of grading properly becomes a question of how students can best learn to judge their own abilities and then put them to effective use. It is in this role that grading is most compatible with the overall objectives of fostering personal growth, competency, and feelings of self-worth.

In Summary

We have argued the necessity of restructuring learning so that it becomes a process of individual goal setting and striving toward manageable objectives. This transformation holds enormous implications for promoting individual excellence and combating failure-avoiding tactics. First and foremost, it acts to alter the definition of success. Success experiences become more a matter of exceeding one's *own* present standards than of surpassing the performance of others. From this other things follow. Success becomes more plentiful and, in theory at least, it does not diminish in reward value despite its greater frequency. As a consequence of increased self-rewards, the need for defensive maneuvering is correspondingly reduced, thereby setting the stage for a success-orientation. This orientation is further promoted by increased school achievement, which is most apt to occur at *all* ability levels whenever students work within their own reach.

Thus, realistic goal setting fosters both increased feelings of success and increasing competency. This combination can set in motion a buoyant, upward cycle in which competency and confidence prosper together. Moreover, tackling work of moderate difficulty acts to strengthen the vital link between effort and outcome. Effort becomes a prime ingredient in attaining one's goals and improper effort the most likely culprit when falling short. This acts to rob failure of much of its threat, even when the failure is preceded by high effort. Other interpretations of failure are now possible besides the self-defeating assumption that, "I am not smart enough."

Over all, then, through a combination of realistic goal setting, task analysis, and proper effort, the pupil's sense of success grows, his actual performance increases, and so does the conviction that he is personally responsible for these changes. This allows for the emergence of a still higher-order value—the importance of individual achievement through effort. And this is the same kind of ethic that teachers hope to encourage. With this alignment of similar objectives, teacher and student are free to engage in a self-fulfilling prophecy of the most positive sort where teachers challenge students to achieve at their best.

Yet there remains another value, coequal to achievement and effort, that of self-acceptance. Realistic goal setting helps here too by providing students with the opportunity to test their limits, for ultimately acceptance of self rests on the ability to accept one's weaknesses as well as one's strengths.

Striving to do things better, yet accepting without rancor the personal limits discovered in this growth process is the essence of the pursuit of individual excellence. Put in terms of the threat to self-worth, it places in perspective society's preoccupation with ability and unbridled achievement as the overriding determinants of human worth.

Although the reader may agree in principle with the analysis presented in this chapter, it may still seem somewhat visionary. Can restructuring the learning process really help all that much? Probably not, if *that* is all we do. Providing students with the structure to strive for excellence is the first necessary step. But the second and equally important step is to provide students with the skills to take full advantage of the opportunity. This second step is the topic of Chapter 6.

General References

Alschuler, A. S., Tabor, D., & McIntyre, J. *Teaching achievement motivation*. Middletown, Conn.: Education Ventures, 1971.

Gardner, J. W. *Excellence: Can we be equal and excellent too?* New York: Harper & Row, 1961.

Kirschenbaum, H., Simon, S., & Napier, R. *Wad-ja-get? The grading game in American education*. New York: Hart, 1971.

Malott, R. *Contingency management in education*. Kalamazoo, Mich.: Behaviordelia, 1972.

Silberman, C. E. *Crisis in the classroom: The remaking of American education*. New York: Vintage Books, 1970.

Chapter 6   Achievement Skills

We have argued the case for student-centered learning on the grounds that it can foster both confidence and competency. Yet restructuring the rules of classroom learning does not automatically guarantee these benefits. Indeed, in at least one case (Alschuler and Ham, 1971) the introduction of individualized goal setting caused an actual *decrease* in school achievement as well as considerable confusion and student resistance. There are two probable causes for such failure.

First, changing the structure of the learning game does not necessarily improve classroom *climate*, and climate is at least as important as *structure* in promoting achievement. Suspicion of teacher motives and distrust among students can linger even after restructuring and thus can interfere with subsequent learning. This is likely to happen because of the deeply ingrained pattern of teacher dominance and student submission, which makes it difficult to turn responsibility over to students even under the best circumstances. In addition, teachers sometimes unwittingly defeat their own purpose by unilaterally changing the rules without first consulting their students or permitting them some voice in shaping the change. Research shows that the quality of work, the degree of pride in the final product, and even one's willingness to undertake the work in the first place, all increase when individuals are taken into the leader's confidence; and that resistance is a common reaction among individuals who are not first consulted about what it is they are to do (de Charms and Bridgeman, 1961; Hammock and Brehm, 1966).

Obviously, then, teacher style affects classroom climate and, in turn, student achievement. As further evidence of this Jacob Kounin (1970) has discovered that student involvement in learning is greatest when teachers arouse student interest, sustain it through novelty and variety in teaching approach, and make students feel accountable for their successes and failures. Such teacher characteristics support a success orientation in the classroom. Happily, there is evidence that teachers can be trained in these and other similar teaching styles, a point that we will consider later in this chapter.

The second factor that weighs against the success of student-centered learning is that many pupils are simply unprepared to take advantage of autonomy and independence. Students who are unable to manage their time and resources properly cannot be expected to complete work contracts successfully, nor can they learn on their own unless they are skilled at evaluating the quality of their own ideas and are able to estimate what they already know in contrast to what they still have to learn. Yet there is every reason to believe that students are universally deficient in precisely these kinds of self-management skills. For example, we know that both children and adults are surprisingly inept at recognizing the best idea for solving a problem even when it appears in a group among other less elegant or even wrong ideas (Covington, 1968; Johnson, Parrott, and Straton, 1968). Moreover, as late as high school and college age many students still cannot tell the difference between really understanding something and not understanding it at all. Such students may press on with an assignment blithely unaware that they are repeating the same mistakes over and over. This is not a matter of inattention; these students are attentive enough. What they lack are the internal checks for testing whether or not their answers fit and are reasonable.

The experimental evidence (see Campbell, 1964) suggests that self-directed learning is effective after, and only after, students are taught good study habits and the skills necessary for autonomous action. Yet countless young people are still cast out—in the name of freedom and creativity—to learn on their own, when and if they wish and without supervision. This inevitably leads to a breakdown of learning, and incidentally is the main reason why the private "free school" movement in America has failed to live up to its promising beginnings. Its philosophy of openness and individuality was admirable; but, according to Jonathan Kozol, one of the original founders of the "free school" movement, no one there learned how to read (Kozol, 1972). Experiments in "nongraded" classrooms in traditional public school settings share the same fate whenever "nongraded" becomes a euphemism for unsupervised learning (Roach, 1975).

Ironically, it is failure-prone students who need autonomy the most yet they are the least able of all students to manage their own learning. To them success is an unexpected event, which they are unable to accept, let alone plan for. They deliberately misjudge their capacity and aspire after irrational goals for defensive purposes, and they are crippled in their problem-solving efforts by anxiety and doubt. Fortunately, there is a growing body of evidence that such self-defeat can be combated through systematic skill training.

The present chapter is divided into three sections. The first deals with research on training students in the skills that underlie the motive to succeed and reviews efforts to help teachers create a classroom climate conducive to the use of these skills. The second section presents research on teaching problem-solving strategies and on the dispositions important to productive thinking. In the final section we will consider training techniques that help students transform anxiety and worry into a more positive motivating force.

Motivation Training

In the mid-1960s David McClelland (1965) asserted that motives could be changed in adulthood through proper training. This was a provocative claim because many psychologists believe that human motives are inherently unchangeable. This is especially true of Freudian psychology, which holds that basic human motives are laid down early in life and that if they are to be changed at all, the change must occur in the very young child. Nonetheless, McClelland offered a set of theoretical guidelines by which such motive change might be accomplished. These propositions have special application to fostering a motive to succeed or, as it is sometimes called, *achievement motivation.*

McClelland's guidelines involve several interrelated learning steps. He reasoned that trainees must first learn to think as success-oriented individuals do. To accomplish this it was suggested that trainees write creative stories about themselves using achievement themes so they might vicariously experience the joy of success and a sense of pride in accomplishment. Doing this, McClelland argued, makes achievement thoughts more salient, and, to the extent that thoughts influence actions, it would presumably promote achievement-like behavior. As a next step, trainees must link these achievement thoughts to achievement behavior. Accordingly, trainees then learn to carry out the sequence of actions implied by achievement striving whenever they confront a problem: identifying the problem, assessing the risks involved, and planning for ways to reduce these risks to acceptable levels. This involves practicing problem-solving strategies in game-like situations before trying to apply them to real life.

McClelland's proposal has stimulated much research. As only one example, several investigators have developed problem-solving games to teach trainees that success depends on a realistic appraisal of personal skills and careful goal-setting in light of the risks. For example, in the "business game" (Litwin and Ciarlo, 1961) players contract to build toy rockets or tractors. Players buy the parts and actually assemble the models. Each player must calculate how many units he can build in the time available. If he underestimates his capacity for work and buys too few parts, he will not make the best use of his time and will therefore incur a loss. Likewise, if he buys too many parts, he will also fail to make a profit. Ingenious materials of this sort have been used to promote achievement motivation among businessmen both in the United States and abroad (Aronoff and Litwin, 1966; Lasker, 1966).

Most pertinent to our interest are studies dealing with school age youngsters. Representative of this research is a study conducted by David Kolb (1965). In this study Kolb administered an achievement motivation course to underachieving high school boys during a six-week summer school. The course involved training in achievement thought patterns, administration of a simplified version of the "business game," and discussions of being planful in striving toward both immediate and long-range goals. After returning to their regular classrooms these students showed significant improvement in their grades when compared with another group of students who had attended the same summer school but were not trained in achievement strategies. This same pattern of improved school grades for underachievers has been found by other investigators, who also report additional positive effects, including a reduction in absenteeism and dropout rates (de Charms, 1968, p. 253; Ryals, 1969). The most encouraging note of all is that students who were initially low in success striving seem to profit most from such training. As Richard de Charms points out (1968, p. 242), these results tend to corroborate McClelland's view that new motives can be established through training. If gains had occurred only among those already high in achievement motivation, then it could be argued that training simply enhanced already existing but latent dispositions and did not build in motives where none existed before.

Similar research has been conducted by de Charms on what he calls *Origin training* (1968). By an *Origin*, de Charms refers to individuals who are in control of their own achievement owing chiefly to their skillful goal setting, planfulness, and readiness to accept personal responsibility for their actions. In contrast, a person is said to be acting as a *Pawn* when he is controlled by others and is helpless and uncertain in the face of outside forces that drive him. Besides characterizing people, de Charms believes that the Origin-Pawn distinction can also be used to describe situations. In some circumstances people are forced to act in predetermined ways by forces beyond their control; at other times, they are freer to decide for themselves and to initiate their own actions. Using the Origin-Pawn concept to describe both people and situations has prompted de Charms to make two basic assertions about school life. First, students will become more involved and motivated if they are treated as Origins rather than as Pawns. Second, Origins will act more productively than Pawns, irrespective of the classroom climate. This reasoning has led to a program of research with a double purpose: to train teachers to treat their students as Origins and to train students to become more Origin-like in their school behavior.

To meet the first of these objectives, de Charms and his associates have developed a brief training course designed to help teachers establish a classroom climate conducive to student self-management. The effects of this training program are assessed through a special questionnaire in which students rate their teachers on a number of Origin dimensions, including the extent to which teachers expect students to take personal responsibility for their own learning, encourage student goal-setting, and instill self-confidence. The results of training are gratifying. In one study, 23 junior high teachers were rated two years after they had completed the training program (de Charms, 1972). Despite this long interval, these teachers were still judged to be significantly more Origin-like in their treatment of students than was a group of comparison teachers who had received no such training. Thus it appears possible to train teachers in these crucial characteristics and—equally important—once established, they become a relatively permanent part of the teacher's instructional style.

Simultaneous with this research on teacher training, Origin training techniques were also developed for students with a special emphasis on learning to take realistic risks. These materials have been used most extensively in studies involving black ghetto children from a large inner city school district (de Charms, 1972). Origin training was administered by regular classroom teachers over a two-year period starting in the sixth grade. Other matched classrooms within the same schools acted as controls. A number of positive changes had occurred by the end of the seventh grade. For one, the trained children were behaving more like Origins in their school work—that is, acting in a more confident, goal-directed manner. For another, these students posted impressive increases in their academic achievement as measured by standardized achievement tests. While the untrained children continued to fall further behind in their grade placement—a common occurrence in ghetto schools—the trained students actually improved slightly in their academic standing.

Since none of the training dealt directly with academic skills, it remains unclear why academic performance improved. The most likely explanation has to do with the benefits of taking moderate risks. As a result of training, the performance standards of these students were brought more in line with their ability to attain them. This doubtlessly led to increased success experiences in school work, which was eventually reflected in higher achievement test scores. This dynamic is essentially the same as that reported by Woodson (see p. 107), who demonstrated that the more congruent the match between current skill level and task difficulty, the greater the resulting achievement for students at all ability levels. This interpretation is also supported by the work of Russell Hill and his colleagues (1974), who found greater convergence between aspirations and ability level among fifth grade students after they were trained in realistic goal-setting; they also showed increased academic achievement.

Interestingly, students who become most congruent as a result of training are those who initially feel the least in control of their own achievement—that is, students with an external locus of control. For example, Dennis Shea (1969) reports that before training, such pupils tend to overestimate what it is they can accomplish. The harder the problem, the more likely they are to try to solve it, with failure the inevitable result. Training helps these students recognize the vital relationship between realistic goal-setting and success. As a result they come to act more like students with an internal locus of control.

At present our best guess is that achievement training acts indirectly to raise academic performance because it improves the pupil's capacity for self-management, especially when it comes to making realistic self-appraisals. Of course, such realism is equally important in fostering self-confidence. Many investigators (see Katz, 1968) believe that confidence is maintained by the positive self-reinforcement that accompanies successful performance. As we have said, the individual who meets or exceeds his standards judges himself in self-approving ways. Achievement training makes such covert reinforcement as favorable as possible by minimizing the difference between self-standards and actual performance. In the larger perspective of promoting mental health, this result is akin to reducing the discrepancy between actual-self and ideal-self. One hopeful sign of our ability to promote student well-being is that failure-avoiding pupils seem to profit most from training. The fact that these students before training habitually strive for unattainable goals, often in a reckless manner, suggests strongly that elements of defensive maneuvering are present. To be able to combat such irrational defensive behaviors and thereby promote self-acceptance—all through the medium of skill training—is a most encouraging development.

However, after a decade of intensive research we are still not certain what it is about motivation training that makes for changes in achievement behavior or whether it is actually motives that are being changed. But undeniably changes do occur. And because of the longevity of these changes and the fact that training affects virtually all aspects of school behavior from rate of absenteeism to grades, it seems likely that researchers have tapped something more profound and enduring than just the surface characteristics of the individual.

Training for Productive Thinking

While some researchers explore the benefits of moderate risk taking, others are investigating the possibility that school achievement can also be improved by training students in the mental or cognitive skills involved in the thinking process. This effort is but one part of a larger contemporary movement in education generally referred to as *process-centered education*, where the emphasis is on teaching students *how* to find "answers" for themselves (see Bruner, 1961; Fair and Shaftel, 1967). The weight of the evidence suggests that training for effective thinking is feasible and that it not only fosters the *ability* to think but increases the student's *willingness* to think as well.

Much of the evidence on these points comes from research on the *Productive Thinking Program*, a course in learning to think for students in the upper elementary grades (Covington *et al.*, 1974). This program consists of a series of complex problems that the student attempts to solve. The content of these problems represents a wide range of contemporary subject-matter topics drawn from the physical and biological sciences, the social sciences, and the humanities. As each problem unfolds page by page, students are given repeated practice in various problem-solving strategies, which include: (1) discovering and formulating problems; (2) organizing and evaluating incoming information; (3) generating many ideas; (4) asking questions in an effective manner; and (5) reformulating problems in new ways. The student practices these strategies as he works through the problem by writing down his ideas, listing questions, and offering suggestions for what next steps to take. Students can judge the appropriateness of their ideas by comparing them with samples of creative responses presented on subsequent pages of the text. In this way the student sharpens his understanding of what constitute appropriate yet ingenious ideas, important questions to ask, and promising lines of investigation.

The results of a number of studies using this program indicate that trained students make substantial improvements in problem-solving performance on a wide range of new problems that differ in content from those used in the training (Covington and Crutchfield, 1965; Olton and Crutchfield, 1969; Ripple and Darcey, 1967). Moreover, most students profit from such training, irrespective of differences in intelligence, social class, and initial levels of thinking proficiency. Nor are such findings limited to this particular research alone. A number of other studies also confirm that training in cognitive skills such as question asking and idea generation can increase problem-solving proficiency in the classroom (Blank and Covington, 1965; Davis, 1970; Feldhusen, Bahlke, and Treffinger, 1969; Suchman, 1966).

But what of the student's *willingness* to think? Improved performance does not guarantee that students will gain sufficient confidence to use their newly won skills. Indeed, we have seen how clever some individuals are at denying their own successes and how apathy so grips others that they become indifferent to intellectual growth and unaware of its meaning and importance. The teaching of any school-related skills—whether they be mental, social, or physical—must proceed in such a manner that proficiency and confidence grow apace. From what we have learned in previous chapters, this requires at least three indispensable conditions: (1) the student must recognize his own progressive improvement; (2) this sense of progress must be accompanied by an actual increase in meaningful success experiences; and (3) the student must come to realize that these successes are under his own personal control through an increasingly *skillful* use of his own *efforts*.

These three elements were built directly into the Productive Thinking Program through the use of identification models. A story line is maintained by developing a narrative concerning two school children. The creative responses given as feedback to the reader are presented as the models' ideas. Thus the student works in concert with the models—the student generating his own questions or ideas, then the models responding with theirs. These models are intended as fictional counterparts of the reader. They are warm, likeable individuals who exhibit strengths as well as weaknesses. Indeed, these models are not perfect. They make mistakes, but they also profit by them and, as a result, they gradually increase both their ability to think and confidence in their ideas. Identification with such realistic models is intended to give the student a sense of his own progressive improvement as a thinker. At the same time, he experiences repeated successes in the face of increasingly more difficult problems in the program. This is accomplished by introducing into each lesson a series of hints and clues to the solution, so that sooner or later every student will be led to solve the problem for himself. The value of these discoveries is heightened by the fact that they are typically made before the problem is solved by the models. Moreover, by being allowed ultimately to succeed after considerable hard work, the link is strengthened between effort and successful outcome, thereby reinforcing the student's image of himself as the cause of his own growing success.

In effect, the use of identification models permits the student to learn more than skills. He can try out for himself what may be a new, unfamiliar role—that of problem-solving expert and thinker; he can unlearn negative attribution patterns; and he can deal with misunderstandings about the nature of thinking and, in particular, learn about the positive benefits of making mistakes. A sample page from the Productive Thinking Program illustrates how such attitudes and values can be strengthened in the context of skill training (see Figure 6.1).

Research based on the Productive Thinking Program suggests that a combination of attitude and skill training can enhance the student's self-confidence in a number of important ways. One index of self-confidence is the student's willingness to use the thinking skills at the risk of failure. In this connection, training increased the likelihood that students would tackle complex problems where success was uncertain, when they just as easily could have avoided any risk by choosing to work on a simple clerical task (Olton and Crutchfield, 1969). Another index of confidence is the degree of independence shown by students in judging the worth of their ideas. Here, trained students were less likely than untrained students to abandon their beliefs simply because they differed from the majority of peer-group opinion (Allen and Levine, 1967). Yet, training did not produce counter-conformers, individuals who automatically reject group opinion simply for the sake of dissent. Rather, these trained students used peer-group opinion selectively, sometimes changing their positions in favor of group opinion and other times rejecting it when they felt *they* and *not* the group were right.

Figure 6.1
A sample page from the Productive Thinking Program

From Covington, M. V., Crutchfield, R. S., Davies, L. B., & Olton, R. M. *The productive thinking program: A course in learning to think.* Columbus, Ohio: Merrill, 1974, pp. 13 and 19. Copyright 1974, The Charles E. Merrill Publishing Co. Reprinted by permission.

A third measure of confidence is the student's own subjective evaluation of himself as a thinker. Here the evidence indicates that trained students came to hold more positive beliefs about thinking and saw themselves as more able to make productive use of their own minds (Olton, 1975; Treffinger and Ripple, 1970).

Anxiety and Anxiety Reduction

While some investigators hope to promote personal excellence by strengthening the dispositions, motives, and intellectual skills that characterize the success-striver, other researchers proceed in an opposite but complementary fashion by attempting to counteract the negative dynamics of the failure-avoiding student. Most of these *remedial* efforts focus on reducing anxiety and its corrosive influence on school performance.

The effect of anxiety on learning is not as simple as one might suppose. For example, anxiety does not always disrupt learning; in fact, sometimes it actually facilitates learning. It all depends on the level of anxiety present, the individual's reaction to threat, and the difficulty of the learning task. Because of this, psychologists have come to distinguish between *facilitative* and *debilitating* anxiety (Alpert and Haber, 1960).

The positive motivating value of anxiety is best seen in the case of low-anxious students. The evidence shows that these students perform best when they are given anxiety-provoking instructions before starting to work on a learning task (see Wine, 1971, p. 96). It appears that some degree of external threat is necessary to mobilize their efforts! In contrast, anxious students perform poorly under the threat of being evaluated. This is especially true in the case of complex learning such as memorizing a spelling list. In fact, for complex tasks the mere presence of anxiety, even in moderate amounts, greatly inhibits performance. However, anxiety benefits performance when the task is easy, such as learning a simple motor response. This relationship between anxiety level, task difficulty, and performance is called the *Yerkes-Dodson Law.*

Since most school learning is quite complicated, it is the threatened student who is most penalized by anxiety. This is well illustrated in the case of complex problem solving where several kinds of performance are necessary, ranging from easy to quite difficult. High-anxious students excel at generating a sheer volume of ideas of indifferent quality (actually a relatively simple achievement), but it is the low-anxious student who is most likely to discover the single best solution to the problem (Covington, 1967). This latter feat is a much more demanding achievement and is the one most often rewarded in school.

In light of all this research it is reasonable to suppose that an optimal degree of arousal is necessary for each individual to achieve at his best and that this optimal level differs dramatically from person to person and from one task to another. Too little arousal may lead to indifference and inaction, whereas too much may doom the student to failure. The key to maintaining an optimal level of arousal for failure-avoiding students is to transform the function of anxiety from debilitation to facilitation—even in the face of threat-provoking situations.

Obviously this is no simple proposition. And, to complicate matters, past research has been badly hampered by an inadequate understanding of precisely how anxiety interferes with learning. Without an adequate theory there is little hope that we can help the anxious student. Indeed, the problem of anxiety illustrates as well as any topic in psychology the fact that there is nothing so practical as a good theory.

Any school child who suffers an anxiety attack can testify to its all-consuming nature, involving as it does, physical agitation, mental worry, and autonomic distress.

This simultaneous bombardment of discomfort from so many sources has made it especially difficult for researchers to identify each of the components of anxiety and to establish their respective roles in causing and sustaining an anxiety attack. Until recently behavioral scientists have blamed the deterioration of learning on emotional upset and autonomic distress, most popularly referred to as "butterflies in the stomach." These are the *arousal* components of anxiety. But now we are beginning to suspect that emotional discomfort is not the main culprit. For one thing, autonomic distress seems to be a natural, almost inevitable, reaction to any situation where a person's performance is being evaluated. Furthermore, emotional arousal is present to about the same extent in both good and poor problem solvers (Spiegler, Morris, and Liebert, 1968). The weight of evidence now points to the *cognitive* or worry component of anxiety as the cause of poor performance. That is, it appears to be the person's troublesome and self-defeating thoughts that interfere with performance. In effect, the anxious student traps himself in what Jeri Wine (1973) calls a "reverberating circuit of worry." He worries that he is falling behind during a test, scolds himself for forgetting the answers, fearfully recalls similar situations that ended in disaster, and above all, he longs to be finished.

In this context anxiety is seen as a response, a reaction to being evaluated. When confronted with a school test, the anxious student reacts with self-doubt, worry, and defensive maneuvering—all triggered by his low expectations for success. This reaction can occur days or even weeks before the dreaded event, and, of course, his prophecy of failure proves only too accurate, foredoomed as the student is by the interfering effects of his own worry and by defensive maneuvering. Autonomic distress, which appears to be of greatest intensity during the actual test, merely aggravates the situation by providing the hapless student with yet another source of distraction. In contrast, the student who faces the test with confidence experiences much the same affective arousal, but for him it becomes motivating owing to the fact that it focuses his attention on the task. It is in this sense that we speak of success-oriented students as being task-oriented.

The shift in emphasis from the arousal components of anxiety to the cognitive elements is a significant one, especially because the various forms of therapy that focus on reducing "emotionality" have not been very successful. There are several reasons for this. For one, it has proven surprisingly difficult to break the learned connection between fear and being evaluated by others. One technique for attempting this is referred to as *desensitization therapy* (Wolpe, 1969). Here the individual is trained to relax as he pictures himself in the presence of progressively more stressful situations: he may imagine himself first merely answering practice questions at the end of a textbook chapter, next studying for a minor quiz, and finally taking an important final examination. In these ways the patient slowly desensitizes himself to the fear-provoking qualities of test taking. But even when the desensitizing process is successful and the individual no longer experiences emotional upset in the face of threat, there is evidence to suggest that performance itself may not improve (Allen, 1972; Wine, 1973). Again, this points to the secondary role of emotional arousal in causing poor performance.

This line of evidence leads to an interesting conclusion: in order to combat the negative aspects of anxiety, failure-avoiding students must be retrained so that self-defeating worry is replaced by task-relevant thought patterns. Once this is done, the arousal components of anxiety can be expected to become facilitating, as is already the case among success-oriented thinkers. A number of studies using such "cognitive retraining" have been conducted in recent years with students ranging from the preschool to the college level. The research of Donald Meichenbaum and Joseph Goodman (1971) illustrates the general principles involved. These investigators encouraged highly impulsive second grade students to talk to themselves as they worked on problems in ways that focused their attention on the task at hand. As a first step, each child observed an adult model work through a problem by giving himself problem-solving instructions aloud—reminding himself to be planful, correcting mistakes, and voicing self-praise for following his own directions. As a next step, the young student worked on the same problem while the adult coached him. From then on, the child worked alone and administered his own instructions, first aloud, then later in a whisper, and finally thinking only to himself. In the space of only a few hours most of these previously impulsive students had brought reflective, problem-solving behavior under internal control.

Such repeated problem-solving practice is also featured in the training of older students, except that, of course, the procedures are modified somewhat to accommodate an increased sophistication and greater capacity for learning. As only one example, Wine (1973) reported training anxious preadolescents to attend to task-relevant factors during test performance. To do this youngsters worked on a variety of intellectual problems, beginning with "game-like" tasks and progressing to "test-like" tasks. Similar step-by-step procedures are used with college students, and in at least one case the training program is self-instructional and presented by computer (Richardson and Grant, 1973).

Thus far, the results of such research are encouraging. Cognitive training reduces excess anxiety in test-taking situations, as does desensitization therapy. But more important, cognitive training alone improves actual test performance. Moreover, these performance gains are found uniformly across all age groups and appear to be quite durable. For instance, Meichenbaum and Goodman (1971) report that their trained students showed a continuing superiority in problem solving over an untrained comparison group for up to four weeks after the original training was completed (at which time the follow-up tests were discontinued).

In Summary

There is clear evidence that the dispositions to strive for success can be broken down into interrelated skill components and trained for in their own right—whether they be realistic goal setting, task analysis, or other problem-solving skills. In addition, strengthening these skills and dispositions has been shown to have a positive effect both on subsequent achievement and on the student's confidence as a learner.

The larger significance of this chapter, however, lies in the implication that skill training must be combined with any restructuring of the learning game before we can expect long-range changes in student autonomy and success orientation. In the long run, the success of student-centered instruction depends on strengthening the underlying skills of autonomy, originality, and independence of thought that sustain it, and, in turn, the exercise of these skills depends on the opportunity to use them.

General References

Covington, M. V., Crutchfield, R. S., Davies, L. B., & Olton, R. M. *The productive thinking program: A course in learning to think.* Columbus, Ohio: Merrill, 1974.

de Charms, R. *Personal causation.* New York: Academic Press, 1968.

McClelland, D. C. Toward a theory of motive acquisition. *American Psychologist*, 1965, **20**, 321–33.

Olton, R. M., & Crutchfield, R. S. Developing the skills of productive thinking. In P. Mussen, J. Langer, & M. V. Covington (Eds.), *Trends and issues in developmental psychology.* New York: Holt, Rinehart and Winston, 1969.

Chapter 7   Epilogue

The student who uses competitive achievement as the test of his worth is in trouble. His belief in himself is too easily threatened, and schools intensify his predicament. This has been one of the central themes in this book. Another vital message is that if students are to overcome the threat of learning, they must be permitted the "freedom to fail." They must feel free to make errors, to ask questions that reveal their (temporary) ignorance, and to risk trying their hardest. Only then can they truly strive for personal excellence. Indeed, when such freedom is granted, the phrase "freedom to fail" becomes almost a misnomer. Failure can more properly be likened to a form of "nonsuccess," and freedom now signals the "freedom to learn."

The phrase, freedom to learn, implies many things, among them: the freedom to readjust one's goals down-

ward if necessary without self-recrimination; freedom from
the incessant fear that each school day brings a new test
of one's worth; and—above all—the freedom to fall short
and, in doing so, to realize that the most terrifying part
of failure is the *anticipation* of failure. Such freedom depends on gaining satisfaction from efforts to achieve one's
own realistic aspirations.

We need not belabor the recommendations made in this
book to promote such freedom by repeating them here,
except in brief form to lend perspective.

First, a number of suggestions have dealt with helping
students organize their own learning, such as dividing
tasks into manageable subparts and clear steps, making
hard tasks easier by analyzing the sources of difficulty, and
setting performance goals in light of one's own progress.
As a result of training in areas such as these, students can
become more task-oriented—focusing on the true obstacles
in the learning process rather than seeing other students
as the obstacles. Moreover, the learner is more likely to
experience feelings of success and attribute them to personal effort. Encouragement becomes the more natural
teacher response, replacing praise with its negative emphasis on extrinsic motivation and dependence on authority.
These benefits are made possible by the restructuring of
the learning game and are sustained in the long run by
systematic training in the skills that promote productive
thinking and that transform anxiety into a more positive
force.

Another cluster of recommendations pertains to the
teacher's role in establishing standards of competency for
students and in helping each student discover adequate and
reasonable achievements for himself. The young student is
particularly receptive—and vulnerable—to the expectations conveyed by the teacher. For this reason the teacher
must be especially sensitive to the kinds of standards that
his students internalize and whether those standards are
realistic. Knowing what is reasonable allows the student
to limit the demands he places on himself—in effect, it puts

a ceiling on failure—so that he is free, if he chooses, to strive beyond mere competency and to chart the full range of his gifts, secure in the knowledge that whatever he finds he is at least adequate. This serves to make the important distinction between competency and talent: not everyone is highly talented, but most are capable of attaining an adequate level of achievement.

In arriving at these recommendations we have had to reassess the nature of success and failure and their roles in learning. As it turns out, success is not uniformly good, as has long been thought, nor is failure always bad. The character of each depends on a number of factors, chief of which are the causes to which students attribute their victories and defeats. Moreover, things are not always as they seem—sometimes to all outward appearances students are highly successful, while in reality, they are threatened and hurting. The overstriver is the classic example of this situation. Success alone never guarantees a sense of personal well-being; to feel good about oneself requires that success be sought out for its own sake and not as a means to avoid failure.

The process of establishing a "freedom to learn" has an almost exact counterpart in the effective child-rearing practices discussed in Chapter 3. You will recall that as a first condition the child must be accepted by his parents for what he is. Teachers, too, must accept their students for what each has achieved thus far, for the potential each brings to the learning place, and for what each can become. Without such unconditional acceptance little learning is possible. To put the point differently, worth resides in each individual as part of his humanness; it is a given, never divisible nor negotiable. When teachers act on this premise, it is less likely that a student's *sense* of worth will suffer. Second, like effective parents, teachers must also set limits of conduct and establish reasonable standards. Every student is capable of responding to some level of excellence and should be held to these standards. And, finally, there is the matter of allowing each student considerable latitude to pursue these standards at his own rate and on his own terms. These three indispensable elements of *acceptance, realistic standards,* and *latitude* for learning are the underpinnings of the recommendations made in this book.

In conclusion, we wonder about the prospects for fostering individual excellence in a society dominated by competitive achievement. It is certainly desirable that individuals learn to recognize their own limits; indeed, as we have argued, this recognition is a necessary although sometimes painful step in building a firm foundation of self-esteem. But what of the student who discovers that he has relatively few, if any, strong points or finds to his dismay that his particular "strengths" are no greater than the "weaknesses" exhibited by the student across the aisle? Can he avoid unfavorable comparisons and content himself with working within his reach, knowing all the while that he is foreclosed from prestigious occupations and status in adulthood owing to his limited gifts? And what of the bright child across the aisle—can *he* find personal satisfaction, blessed as he is with the burden and responsibility of extraordinary talent?

We raised essentially these same questions in the introductory chapter when we quoted John Gardner (1961) asking whether it is possible to teach so that ". . . individuals at every [intellectual] level will realize their full potentialities, perform at their best and harbor no resentment toward any other level?"

Gardner's question cannot be answered in the abstract nor for all time but only with regard to individual students and teachers in specific classrooms. Considering the question at this level, there is reason to be optimistic about combating resentment. Being aware of a problem and willing to work to create change brings solutions that much closer. And, as this book indicates, we understand a good deal about the effects of unbridled competition, fear of failure, and the threat of learning, and in theory about how to check these excesses. Yet we must be realistic. Resentment is an inevitable outcome of schooling; it cannot be banished, only moderated and hopefully before it destroys the individual's will to learn. There are two reasons for this hard core of resentment. One has to do with the role of schools in society and the other with the limited power of schools as agents of social reform. As to the first of these, in reality schools sort out students as well as teach them; students who learn quickest are selected to learn more and thereby prosper in a society that values high educational attainments. The results of this sorting out process are disappointed hopes, anguish, and resentment among those who do not reach the "top."

The other source of resentment stems from exaggerated claims by some reformers that schools can solve our social ills. When schools do not deliver on these promises, the public is disillusioned and resentment again results, especially among minority groups who see education as a way to a better life. An especially pertinent example of this was the reform movement of the late 1960s whose proponents argued that increasing the quality of education for all children—in effect, equalizing educational opportunity—would reduce economic inequality in the next generation. Christopher Jencks and his colleagues (1972) attack this claim as Utopian. They conclude that even if schools could somehow manage to equalize cognitive skills among all children, this still would not significantly reduce the gap between the highest-paid and the lowest-paid income groups in our country because, as they argue, these inequalities of income depend primarily on other factors such as luck, family background, and temperament. These, of course, are variables over which schools exert no direct control. Whether or not Jencks and his associates are correct in their analysis, it does serve to remind us that schools as a force for social good are limited in what they can accomplish. To pretend otherwise is the cruelest deception. Similarly, no one can reasonably expect that by restructuring school learning we will totally neutralize the harmful effects of cut-throat competition or offset society's reliance on competitive achievement as its dominant criterion of human worth. But Jencks's analysis does suggest something about the true mission of schools. As he points out, schools must be places that value ideas and the productive use of the mind, not because doing so will automatically guarantee social justice but for the sake of enriching individual lives. First and foremost our schools should honor personal excellence—at all levels of society and in every kind of work where feelings of well-being are supported by the individual reaching for the kinds of excellence within his grasp. Nowhere is this point made with such wry wit and force as when John Gardner remarks,

An excellent plumber is infinitely more admirable than an incompetent philosopher. The society which scorns excellence in plumbing because plumbing is a humble activity and tolerates shoddiness in philosophy because it is an exalted activity will have neither good plumbing nor good philosophy. Neither its pipes nor its theories will hold water [1961, p. 86].

General References

Gardner, J. W. *Self-renewal*. New York: Harper & Row, 1965.

Holt, J. *How children learn*. New York: Dell, 1967.

Jencks, C., Smith, M., Acland, H., Bane, M. J., Cohen, D., Gintis, H., Heyns, B., & Michelson, S. *Inequality*. New York: Harper & Row, Harper Colophon Books, 1972.

References

Allen, G. J. The behavioral treatment of test anxiety. *Behavior Therapy*, 1972, **3**, 253–62.

Allen, V. L., & Levine, J. M. Creativity and conformity. Technical Report No. 33, 1967. Madison, Wisconsin: University of Wisconsin Research and Development Center for Cognitive Learning.

Alpert, R., & Haber, R. N. Anxiety in academic achievement situations. *Journal of Abnormal and Social Psychology*, 1960, **61**, 207–15.

Alschuler, A. S. The effects of classroom structure on achievement motivation and academic performance. *Educational Technology*, 1969, **IX**, 19–24.

Alschuler, A. S. *Developing achievement motivation in adolescents*. New Jersey: Educational Technology Publications, 1973a.

Alschuler, A. S. Toward a humanist discipline. Unpublished manuscript, University of Massachusetts, 1973b.

Alschuler, A. S. Radical psychological education. Keynote Address at the convention of the Virginia Personnel and Guidance Association, Williamsburg, Virginia, March 1975.

Alschuler, A. S., & Ham, M. The motivational impact of individualized instruction. Chapter 6 in Achievement motivation development project, Final Report, Office of Education, Bureau of Research, 1971.

Alschuler, A. S., & Shea, J. V. *The discipline game:* Playing without losers. *Learning Magazine*, August–September, 1974.

Alschuler, A. S., Tabor, D., & McIntyre, J. *Teaching achievement motivation*. Middletown, Conn.: Education Ventures, 1971.

Anderson, D. G. Self-assigned grades. *Counselor Education and Supervision*. Fall 1966, **6**, 75–76.

Anderson, H. H., & Brandt, H. F. Study of motivation involving self-announced goals of fifth grade children and the concept of level of aspiration. *Journal Social Psychology*, 1939, **10**, 209–32.

Aronfreed, J. The origin of self-criticism. *Psychological Review*, 1964, **71**, 193–218.

Aronoff, J., & Litwin, G. H. Achievement motivation training and executive advancement. Unpublished paper, Harvard University, 1966.

Aronson, E., & Carlsmith, J. M. Performance expectancy as a determinant of actual performance. *Journal of Abnormal and Social Psychology*, 1962, **65**, 178–82.

Aronson, E., & Mettee, D. R. Dishonest behavior as a function of differential levels of induced self-esteem. *Journal of Personality and Social Psychology*, 1968, **9**, 121–27.

Atkinson, J. W., & Litwin, G. H. Achievement motive and test anxiety conceived as motive to approach success and motive to avoid failure. *Journal of Abnormal and Social Psychology*, 1960, **60**, 52–63.

Bandura, A. Social learning theory. New York: General Learning Press. 1971. Pp. 1–46.

Bandura, A., Grusec, J. E., & Menlove, F. L. Some determinants of self-monitoring reinforcement systems. *Journal of Personality and Social Psychology*, 1967, **5**, 449–55.

Bandura, A., & Kupers, C. J. Transmission of patterns of self-reinforcement through modeling. *Journal of Abnormal and Social Psychology*, 1964, **69**, 1–9.

Barker, R. G. Two—Success and failure in the classroom. *Progressive Education*, 1942, **19**, 221–24.

Battle, E. S. Motivational determinants of academic task persistence. *Journal of Personality and Social Psychology*, 1965, **2**, 209–18.

Battle, E. S. Motivational determinants of academic competence. *Journal of Personality and Social Psychology*, 1966, **4**, 634–42.

Battle, E., & Rotter, J. B. Children's feelings of personal control as related to social class and ethnic group. *Journal of Personality*, 1963, **31**, 482–90.

Beckman, L. J. Effects of students' performance on teachers' and observers' attributions of causality. *Journal of Educational Psychology*, 1970, **61**, 76–82.

Beery, R. G. Fear of failure. In T. Winnett (Ed.) *Social psychology*. Berkeley, Cal.: Fybate Lecture Notes, 1971.

Beery, R. G. An attributional analysis of student motivation to avoid failure. Paper presented in Symposium: Fostering student motivation and satisfaction in the college classroom, at the meeting of the Western Psychological Association, San Francisco, 1974.

Beery, R. G. Fear of failure in the student experience. *Personnel and Guidance Journal*, 1975, **54**, 190–203.

Berger, E. M. Willingness to accept limitations and college achievement. *Journal of Counseling Psychology*, 1961, **8**, 140–46.

Birney, R. C., Burdick, H., & Teevan, R. C. *Fear of failure*. New York: Van Nostrand, 1969.

Blank, S. S., & Covington, M. V. Inducing children to ask questions in solving problems. *Journal of Educational Research*, 1965, **59**, 21–27.

Bricklin, B., & Bricklin, P. M. *Bright child—Poor grades*. New York: Dell, 1967.

Brock, T. C. Implications of commodity theory for value change. In A. G. Greenwald, T. C. Brock, & T. M. Ostrom (Eds.), *Psychological foundations of attitudes*, New York: Academic Press, 1968.

Bruner, J. S. *The process of education*. Cambridge: Harvard University Press, 1961.

Butterfield, E. C. Locus of control, test anxiety, reactions to frustration, and achievement attitudes. *Journal of Personality*, 1964, **32**, 298–311.

Campbell, V. N. Self-direction and programmed instruction for five different types of learning objectives. *Psychology in The Schools*, 1964, **I**, 348–59.

Campeau, P. L. Test anxiety and feedback in programmed instruction. *Journal of Experimental Psychology*, 1968, **59**, 159–63.

Casady, M. The tricky business of giving rewards. *Psychology Today*, 1974, **8**, 52.

Chamberlin, D., Chamberlin, E. S., Drought, N. E., & Scott, W. E. *Adventures in American education: Did they succeed in college?* New York: Harper & Brothers, 1942.

Child, I. L., & Whiting, J. W. Determinants of level of aspiration: Evidence from everyday life. *Journal of Abnormal Psychology*, 1949, **44**, 303–14.

Clark, K. *Civilisation*. New York: Harper & Row, 1969.

Cohen, J., & Filipczak, J. *A new learning environment*. San Francisco: Jossey-Bass, 1971.

Cook, R. Relation of achievement motivation and attribution to self-reinforcement. Unpublished doctoral dissertation, University of California, Los Angeles, 1970.

Cook, S. W. A survey of methods used to produce experimental neurosis. *American Journal of Psychiatry*, 1939, **95**, 1259–76.

Coopersmith, S. *The antecedents of self-esteem.* San Francisco and London: Freeman, 1967.

Coopersmith, S., & Feldman, R. Fostering a positive self-concept and high self-esteem in the classroom. In R. H. Coop & K. White (Eds.), *Psychological concepts in the classroom.* New York: Harper & Row, 1974.

Covington, M. V. The effects of anxiety on various types of ideational output measures in complex problem solving. Paper presented at the meeting of the Western Psychological Association, San Francisco, 1967.

Covington, M. V. Promoting creative thinking in the classroom. In H. J. Klausmeier & G. T. O'Hearn (Eds.), *Research and development toward the improvement of education.* Madison, Wisc.: December Educational Research Services, 1968, 22–30.

Covington, M. V., & Crutchfield, R. S. Experiments in the use of programmed instruction for the facilitation of creative problem solving. *Programmed Instruction,* 1965, **4**, 3–5, 10.

Covington, M. V., Crutchfield, R. S., Davies, L. B., & Olton, R. M. *The productive thinking program: A course in learning to think.* Columbus, Ohio: Merrill, 1974.

Covington, M. V., & Jacoby, K. E. *Thinking psychology: Student projects, Sets I and II.* Berkeley: Institute of Personality Assessment and Research, University of California, 1972.

Covington, M. V., & Jacoby, K. E. Productive thinking and course satisfaction as a function of an independence-conformity dimension. Paper presented at the meeting of the American Psychological Association, Montreal, 1973.

Covington, M. V., & Omelich, C. L. Fear of failure, attributions and the role of effort. Unpublished manuscript, Institute of Personality Assessment and Research, University of California, Berkeley, 1975.

Covington, M. V., & Polsky, S. Introduction to the program of research: The Berkeley *Teaching-Learning Project.* Paper presented in Symposium: Fostering student motivation and satisfaction in the college classroom, at the meeting of the Western Psychological Association, San Francisco, 1974.

Davids, A., & Hainsworth, P. K. Maternal attitudes about family life and child rearing as avowed by mothers and perceived by their underachieving and high-achieving sons. *Journal of Consulting Psychology*, 1967, **31**, 29–37.

Davis, G. A. Problems in assessing the effectiveness of creative thinking. Paper presented in Symposium: Assessing creativity: Progress in both directions, at the meeting of the American Educational Research Association, Minneapolis, 1970.

de Charms, R. *Personal causation*. New York: Academic Press, 1968.

de Charms, R. Personal causation training in the schools. *Journal of Applied Social Psychology*, 1972, **2**, 95–113.

de Charms, R., & Bridgeman, W. J. Leadership compliance and group behavior. Technical Report No. 9, 1961, Washington University, St. Louis, Mo., ONR Project Nonr 816 (11).

Diggory, J. C. *Self-evaluation: Concepts and studies*. New York: John Wiley & Sons, 1966.

Dweck, C. S. The role of expectations and attributions in the alleviation of learned helplessness. *Journal of Personality and Social Psychology*, 1975, **31**, 674–85.

Dweck, C. S., & Reppucci, N. D. Learned helplessness and reinforcement responsibility in children. *Journal of Personality and Social Psychology*, 1973, **25**, 109–16.

Epstein, S. The self-concept revisited or a theory of a theory. *American Psychologist*, 1973, **28**, 404–16.

Fair, J., & Shaftel, F. R. Effective thinking in the social studies. National Council for the Social Studies, 37th Yearbook. Washington, D.C.: National Education Association, 1967.

Feldhusen, J. F., Bahlke, S. J., & Treffinger, D. J. Teaching creative thinking. *Elementary School Journal*, 1969, **70**, 48–53.

Felsenthal, H. M. Sex differences in teacher-pupil interactions and their relationship with teacher attitudes and pupil reading achievement. *Dissertation Abstracts*, 1970, **30** [9-A,] 3781–82.

Flowers, J. V. The effect of self-reinforcement and self-punishment on test performance in elementary school children. Paper presented at the meeting of the Western Psychological Association, San Francisco, 1974.

Fromkin, H. L., & Brock, T. C. Erotic materials: A commodity theory analysis of the enhanced desirability that may accompany their unavailability. *Journal of Applied Social Psychology*, 1973, **3**, 219–31.

Gagné, R. M. *Essentials of learning instruction.* Hinsdale, Ill.: Dryden Press, a division of Holt, Rinehart and Winston, 1974.

Gardner, J. W. *Excellence: Can we be equal and excellent too?* New York: Harper & Row, 1961.

Gardner, J. W. *Self-renewal.* New York: Harper & Row, 1965.

Gergen, K. J. *The concept of self.* New York: Holt, Rinehart and Winston, 1971.

Gilmore, J. V. *The productive personality.* San Francisco: Albion Publishing, 1974.

Goldberg, L. R. Grades as motivants. *Psychology in The Schools*, 1965, **II**, 17–24.

Goldenberg, I. I. Reading groups and some aspects of teacher behavior. In F. Kaplan & S. B. Sarason (Eds.), *The psycho-educational clinic: Papers on research studies.* Boston: Dept. of Mental Health, Commonwealth of Massachusetts, 1969.

Gould, R. An experimental analysis of "Level of aspiration." *Genetic Psychology Monographs*, 1939, **21**, 1–116.

Grimes, J. W., & Allinsmith, W. Compulsivity, anxiety, and school achievement. *Merrill-Palmer Quarterly*, 1961, **7**, 247–72.

Hammock, T., & Brehm, J. W. The attractiveness of choice alternatives when freedom to choose is eliminated by a social agent. *Journal of Personality*, 1966, **34**, 546–54.

Harrison, R. Classroom innovation. In P. J. Runkel,

R. Harrison, & M. Runkel (Eds.), *The changing college classroom*. San Francisco: Jossey-Bass, 1969.

Heider, F. *The psychology of interpersonal relations*. New York: Wiley, 1958.

Henry, J. Attitude organization in elementary school classrooms. *American Journal of Orthopsychiatry*. 1957, **27**, 117–33.

Hilgard, E. R., Sait, E. M., & Magaret, G. A. Level of aspiration as affected by relative standing in an experimental social group. *Journal Experimental Psychology*, 1940, **27**, 411–21.

Hill, R. A. Achievement competency training: A final report, 1974. Philadelphia: Humanizing Learning Program, Research for Better Schools, 1974.

Holt, J. *How children fail*. New York: Dell, 1964.

Holt, J. *How children learn*. New York: Dell, 1967.

Homme, L. *How to use contingency contracting in the classroom*. Champaign, Ill.: Research Press, 1970.

Horner, M. S. Toward an understanding of achievement-related conflicts in women. *Journal of Social Issues*, 1972, **28**, 157–75.

Jackson, P. W. Alienation in the classroom. *Psychology in Schools*, 1965, **II**, 299–308.

Jackson, P. W. *Life in classrooms*. New York: Holt, Rinehart and Winston, 1968.

Jencks, C., Smith, M., Acland, H., Bane, M. J., Cohen, D., Gintis, H., Heyns, B., & Michelson, S. *Inequality*. New York: Harper & Row, Harper Colophon Books, 1972.

Johnson, D. M., Parrott, G. L., & Stratton, R. P. Production and judgment of solutions to five problems. *Journal of Educational Psychology*, 1968, **59** (Monogr. Suppl. 6).

Johnson, T. J., Feigenbaum, R., & Weiby, M. Some determinants and consequences of the teacher's perception of causation. *Journal of Educational Psychology*, 1964, **55**, 237–46.

Jones, S. C. Self- and interpersonal evaluations: Esteem

theories versus consistency theories. *Psychological Bulletin*, 1973, **79**, 185–99.

Katz, I. Academic motivation and equal educational opportunity. *Harvard Educational Review*, 1968, **38**, 57–65.

Kennedy, W. A., & Willcutt, H. C. Praise and blame as incentives. *Psychological Bulletin*, 1964, **62**, 323–32.

Kindsvatter, R. Guidelines for better grading. *The Clearing House*, 1969, **43**, 331–37.

Kirschenbaum, H., Simon, S., & Napier, R. *Wad-ja-get? The grading game in American education*. New York: Hart, 1971.

Kolb, D. A. Achievement motivation training for underachieving high school boys. *Journal of Personality and Social Psychology*, 1965, **2**, 783–92.

Kounin, J. S. *Discipline and group management in classrooms*. New York: Holt, Rinehart and Winston, 1970.

Kozol, J. *Free Schools*. Boston: Houghton Mifflin, 1972.

LaBenne, W. D., & Greene, B. I. *Educational implications of self-concept theory*. Pacific Palisades, Cal.: Goodyear Publishing Co., 1969.

Lanzetta, J. T., & Hannah, T. E. Reinforcing behavior of "naive" trainers. *Journal of Personality and Social Psychology*, 1969, **11**, 245–52.

Lasker, H. M. Factors affecting responses to achievement motivation training in India. Unpublished honors thesis, Harvard College, 1966.

Lefcourt, H. M. Internal versus external control of reinforcement: A review. *Psychological Bulletin*, 1966, **65**, 206–20.

Lepper, M. R., Greene, D., & Nisbett, R. E. Undermining children's intrinsic interest with extrinsic rewards. *Journal of Personality and Social Psychology*, 1973, **28**, 129–37.

Lepper, M. R., & Greene, D. Turning play into work: Effects of adult surveillance and extrinsic rewards on children's intrinsic motivation. *Journal of Personality and Social Psychology*, 1975, **31**, 479–86.

Lewin, K., Dembo, T., Festinger, L., & Sears, P. Level of

aspiration. In J. McV. Hunt (Ed.), *Personality and the behavior disorders.* Vol. 1. New York: Ronald, 1944.

Litwin, G. H., & Ciarlo, J. A. Achievement motivation and risk-taking in a business setting. Technical Report. New York: General Electric Company, Behavioral Research Service, 1961.

Locke, E. A. Toward a theory of task motivation and incentives. *Organizational Behavior and Human Performance*, 1968, **3**, 157–89.

Lovitt, T. C., & Curtiss, K. A. Academic response rate as a function of teacher- and self-imposed contingencies. *Journal of Applied Behavior Analysis*, 1969, **2**, 49–53.

Marecek, J., & Mettee, D. R. Avoidance of continued success as a function of self-esteem, level of esteem certainty, and responsibility for success. *Journal of Personality and Social Psychology*, 1972, **22**, 98–107.

Marso, R. N. The influence of test difficulty upon study efforts and achievement. *American Educational Research Journal*, 1969, **6**, 621–32.

Marston, A. R. Dealing with low self-confidence. *Educational Research* (Great Britain), 1968, **10**, 134–38.

Martire, J. G. Relationships between the self-concept and differences in the strength and generality of achievement motivation. *Journal of Personality*, 1956, **24**, 364–75.

Masters, J. C. Effects of social comparison upon children's self-reinforcement and altruism toward competitors and friends. *Developmental Psychology*, 1971, **5**, 64–72.

McClelland, D. C. Toward a theory of motive acquisition. *American Psychologist*, 1965, **20**, 321–33.

McClelland, D. C. What is the effect of achievement motivation training in the schools? *Teachers College Record*, 1972, **74**, 129–45.

Meichenbaum, D. H., & Bowers, K. S. A behavioral analysis of teacher expectancy effect. *Journal of Personality and Social Psychology*, 1969, **13**, 306–16.

Meichenbaum D. H., & Goodman, J. Training impulsive children to talk to themselves. *Journal of Abnormal Psychology*, 1971, **77**, 115–26.

Mettee, D. R. Rejection of unexpected success as a function of the negative consequences of accepting success. *Journal of Personality and Social Psychology*, 1971, **17**, 332–41.

Meunier, C., & Rule, B. G. Anxiety, confidence and conformity. *Journal of Personality*, 1967, **35**, 498–504.

Mischel, W., & Liebert, R. M. Effects of discrepancies between observed and imposed reward criteria on their acquisition and transmission. *Journal of Personality and Social Psychology*, 1966, **3**, 45–53.

Nelson, L. L., & Kagan, S. Competition: The star-spangled scramble. *Psychology Today*, 1972, 53–56, 90–91.

Noll, J. O. An investigation of the relation of anxiety to learning and retention. *Dissertation Abstracts*, 1955, **15**.

Odell, M. Personality correlates of independence and conformity. Unpublished master's thesis, Ohio State University, 1959.

Olton, R. S. Personal communication, 1975.

Olton, R. M., & Crutchfield, R. S. Developing the skills of productive thinking. In P. Mussen, J. Langer, & M. V. Covington (Eds.), *Trends and issues in developmental psychology*. New York: Holt, Rinehart and Winston, 1969.

Omelich, C. L. Attribution and achievement in the classroom: The self-fulfilling prophecy. Paper presented at the meeting of the California Personnel and Guidance Association, San Francisco, 1974a.

Omelich, C. L. Control beliefs and school-related attitudes, behavior, and achievement among high school males of four ethnic groups in California. Unpublished manuscript, School of Education, University of California, Berkeley, 1974b.

Osborne, J. G. Free-time as a reinforcer in the management of classroom behavior. *Journal of Applied Behavior Analysis*, 1969, **2**, 113–18.

Page, E. Teacher comments and student performance. *Journal of Educational Psychology*, 1958, **49**, 173–81.

Paterson, D. The conservation of human talent, Walter Van Dyke Bingham Lecture, Ohio State University, 1956.

Pepitone, A., Faucheux, C., Moscovici, S., Cesa-Bianchi, M., Magistretti, G., & Iacono, G. The role of self-esteem in competitive behavior. Unpublished manuscript, University of Pennsylvania, 1969.

Purky, W. W. *Self concept and school achievement.* Englewood Cliffs, N.J.: Prentice-Hall, 1970.

Rest, S., Nierenberg, R., Weiner, B., & Heckhausen, H. Further evidence concerning the effects of perceptions of effort and ability on achievement evaluation. *Journal of Personality and Social Psychology*, 1973, **28**, 187–91.

Richardson, F. C., & Grant. A self-study manual on coping with test anxiety. Technical Report, Computer-Assisted Instruction Laboratory, The University of Texas at Austin, 1973.

Ripple, R. E., & Darcey, J. The facilitation of problem solving and verbal creativity by exposure to programmed instruction. *Psychology in the Schools*, 1967, **4**, 240–45.

Rist, R. C. Student social class and teacher expectations: The self-fulfilling prophecy in ghetto education. *Harvard Educational Review*, 1970, **40**, 411–50.

Roach, M. C. Personal communication, 1975.

Rosen, B. C., & D'Andrade R. The psychosocial origins of achievement motivation. *Sociometry*, 1959, **22**, 185–218.

Rosenberg, J. *Society and the adolescent self-image.* Princeton, N.J.: Princeton University Press, 1965.

Rotter, J. B. Generalized expectancies for internal versus external control of reinforcement. *Psychological Monographs: General and Applied*, 1966, **80**, 1–28.

Rowe, M. Wait-time and rewards as instructional variables: Their influence on language, logic, and fate-control. Paper presented at the meeting of the National Association for Research in Science Teaching, 1972.

Rubin, S. E. Personal Communication, 1975. Also *Newsweek*, Feb. 10, 1975, 44.

Ryals, K. R. An experimental study of achievement motivation training as a function of the moral maturity of trainees. Unpublished doctoral dissertation, Washington University, St. Louis, Mo., 1969.

Schnur, A. E. Fear of failure, effort motive, and student satisfaction in the college classroom. Paper presented at the meeting of the Western Psychological Association, Sacramento, 1975.

Sears, P. S. Levels of aspiration in academically successful and unsuccessful children. *Journal of Abnormal and Social Psychology*, 1940, **35**, 498–536.

Seligman, M. E. P., Maier, S. F., & Geer, J. H. Alleviation of learned helplessness in the dog. *Journal of Abnormal Psychology*, 1968, **73**, 256–62.

Shaw, M. C., & McCuen, J. T. The onset of academic under-achievement in bright children. *Journal of Educational Psychology*, 1960, **51**, 103–8.

Shea, D. J. The effects of achievement motivation training on motivational and behavioral variables. Unpublished doctoral dissertation, Washington University, St. Louis, Mo., 1969.

Shelton, J., & Hill, J. Effects on cheating of achievement anxiety and knowledge of peer performance. *Developmental Psychology*, 1969, **1**, 449–55.

Silberman, C. E. *Crisis in the classroom: The remaking of American education.* New York: Vintage Books, 1970.

Spiegler, M. D., Morris, L. W., & Liebert, R. M. Cognitive and emotional components of test anxiety: Temporal factors. *Psychological Reports*, 1968, **22**, 451–56.

Strom, R. D., & Torrance, E. P. *Education for affective achievement.* New York: Rand McNally & Co., 1973.

Suchman, R. J. *Inquiry development program: Resource book.* Chicago: Science Research Associates, 1966.

Taylor, H. *How to change colleges: Notes on radical reform.* New York: Holt, Rinehart and Winston, 1971.

Teevan, R. C., & Fischer, R. Hostile press and childhood reinforcement patterns: A replication. Unpublished manuscript, Lewisburg, Pa.: Bucknell University, 1967.

Treffinger, D. J., & Ripple, R. E. Programmed instruction in creative problem solving: An interpretation of recent research findings. Mimeographed. Lafayette, Ind.: Purdue University, 1970.

Wardrop, J. L., Goodwin, W. L., Klausmeier, H. J., Olton, R. M., Covington, M. V., Crutchfield, R. S., & Ronda, T. Developing productive thinking skills in fifth-grade students. *Journal of Experimental Education*, 1969, **37**, 67–77.

Weiner, B. Attribution theory, achievement motivation, and the educational process. *Review of Educational Research*, 1972, **42**, 203–15.

Weiner, B., Frieze, I., Kukla, A., Reed, L., Rest, S., & Rosenbaum, R. Perceiving the causes of success and failure. In E. E. Jones (Ed.), *Attribution: Perceiving the causes of behavior*. New York: General Learning Press, 1971.

Weiner, B., & Kukla, A. An attributional analysis of achievement motivation. *Journal of Personality and Social Psychology*, 1970, **15**, 1–20.

Weiner, B., & Peter, N. V. A cognitive-developmental analysis of achievement and moral judgements. *Developmental Psychology*, 1973, **9**, 290–309.

Weinstein, R. S. Personal Communication, 1975.

White, M. A. The view from the pupil's desk. *The Urban Review*, 1968, **2**, 5–7.

Wine, J. Test anxiety and direction of attention. *Psychological Bulletin*, 1971, **76**, 92–104.

Wine, J. Cognitive-attentional approches to test anxiety modification. Paper presented in Symposium: Anxiety and instruction, at the meeting of the American Psychological Association, Montreal, 1973.

Wolpe, J. *The practice of behavior therapy*. New York: Pergamon, 1969.

Woodson, C. E. Motivational effects of two-stage testing. Unpublished manuscript, Institute of Human Learning, University of California, Berkeley, 1975.

Index